JAN - 9 2024

# PRAISE FOR
# *THE SCREENTIME SOLUTION*

"You can love YouTube, Netflix, and Wordle and *still* want your kids to spend a bigger chunk of their time interacting with friends, nature, and the neighborhood IRL. This book is a simple, straightforward life manual for those of us realistic enough to realize tech is not all bad . . . but that there is *something* bad about too much tech, too soon."

—**LENORE SKENAZY**, author of *Free-Range Kids* and president of Let Grow

"Raising thriving kids in today's highly digital world requires a new set of tools that deals with the very real challenges presented by social media and ubiquitous screentime. Emily Cherkin's *The Screentime Solution* provides parents those tools in a nonjudgmental, honest, and practical way. Every family needs this book."

—**MICHELE BORBA, EDD**, best-selling author of *Thrivers* and *UnSelfie*

"Mentoring kids in our tech-saturated world can be confusing and sometimes isolating—despite the fact that everyone is in the same boat. Parents seeking pragmatic approaches and empathy for the challenges of parenting in the digital age will find a welcome perspective in Cherkin's book."

—**DEVORAH HEITNER, PhD**, author of *Growing Up in Public* and *Screenwise*

"Emily provides a realistic and judgment-free guide to parenting in the digital age. A good read for parents scrambling to keep up with the chaos of raising a child in today's world."

—**MAX STOSSEL**, CEO of Social Awakening

"A thoughtful, readable, compassionate guide for parents struggling to cope with the tech industry's relentless, unethical, and profit-driven efforts to capture and hold children's hearts and minds."

—SUSAN LINN, EdD, author of *Who's Raising the Kids: Big Tech, Big Business, and the Lives of Children*

"She had me at the first sentence. Teachers who are also parents offer a unique perspective on reconciling technology with what children really need, and Cherkin's new book does not disappoint. Readers will appreciate her warmth, insight, and clear guidance."

—VICTORIA L. DUNCKLEY, MD, child psychiatrist, screentime expert, and author of *Reset Your Child's Brain*

"Emily Cherkin gives parents what they crave—research-based information and practical tools on how to be 'tech-intentional.' From years of experience as a teacher, parent, and consultant, she explains why screentime is so addictive and offers innovative ideas to help us and our children use technology appropriately. This eye-opening book is a must-read for parents and educators who desire a healthier world."

—ANNE GREEN GILBERT, creator of BrainDance™

"Emily Cherkin's *The Screentime Solution* is a meaningful resource to help build awareness of how technology can steal time from childhood development, relationships, and experiences. For parents, teachers, and anyone that interacts with children of any age, Ms. Cherkin gives insights with delightful verbiage to guide littles and middles to understand, and tips for grown-ups. If you have too much on your plate, read the TL;DRs!"

—NANCY TORGERSON, optometrist, author of *The Essential Playbook*: *How to Maximize Outcomes in Optometric Vision Therapy*

"Tired of fighting with your kids about tech use? Ready to be intentional instead of reactive? *The Screentime Solution* is for you. Emily Cherkin is both The Screentime Consultant *and* a mom. She writes from the trenches. No guilt, no shame. No unrealistic rules. And she's writing to you."

—RHONDA MOSKOWITZ, founder of
Practical Solutions Parent Coaching

"*The Screentime Solution* belongs on every parent's bookshelf. From expecting first-timers to seasoned veterans, Emily Cherkin dispenses timeless advice that parents can return to year after year as their children grow and their family's relationships with screens change."

—ANDY LIDDELL, attorney, digital rights advocate,
and cofounder of the Student Data Privacy Project

"A brave, practical, and thoughtful guide to parenting in the digital age."

—BLYTHE WINSLOW, cofounder and executive
director of Everyschool.org

"Parents are in a difficult position—they are required to parent in today's world with knowledge they gained years ago. This can too often lead parents to feel powerless, whereas nothing could be further from the truth. Emily Cherkin gives information that can help parents to be more effective in helping their children negotiate this new world."

—DOUGLAS A. GENTILE, PhD, distinguished
professor in liberal arts and sciences, Department of
Psychology, Iowa State University

"With immense compassion for both children and parents, Emily Cherkin's *The Screentime Solution* arrives in a time of our cultural crisis, created by the dynamic presence of technology and its devices, in all domains of our daily lives. While recognizing the value of these devices as tools for all of us, Emily deftly names how they also jeopardize the mental health and development of children, while challenging parents in unprecedented ways in their care and protection of their children. Emily is a seasoned educator, a parent of two children, an expert in her field, and a master communicator. With this book, she provides parents with empowering insights and effective interventions and strategies, anchored in the overarching importance of evolving secure adult relations with each child throughout the arc of her and his development. This book is an extraordinary, timely gift that will keep on giving!"

—RICK MEYER, LMHC, MEd

"The feelings I had when reading Emily Cherkin's *The Screentime Solution* were not what I expected. I had expected to feel overwhelmed and scared about my kids and parenting mistakes. Instead, I felt validated, relieved, and empowered. Emily is a parent, educator, and advocate; all three roles influence her practical, compassionate guidance. As a psychologist, I deeply appreciated Emily's supportive, baby-steps approach to making lasting changes in our relationship with screens. For any parent or caregiver struggling with conflicts with children over screentime or worried about what excessive screentime is doing to children, there is no better guide than this one to find a way out."

—ELIZABETH MORRISON, PhD, LCSW,
psychologist and licensed clinical social worker

"Emily's book is a realistic, pragmatic approach for families to use when handling screentime issues. Screen use is part of our world, for better and worse. Emily's work absolutely helps families maximize the 'better' and minimize the 'worse.' Her common sense, judgment-free ideas, and wisdom are enormously important for every family today."

—MATT MILES and JOE CLEMENT, public school
teachers and coauthors of *Screen Schooled*

"There is really no other way to manage screen time. Emily's tech-intentional methodology helps families ask the right questions and easily make difficult decisions based on values and outcomes. *The Screentime Solution* reveals what screens and play meant to prior generations, empowering parents to preserve childhood while raising a generation that will never know a world without the internet. This book gives parents the strength and the tools to not just 'give in or give up.' *The Screentime Solution* honors different family scenarios and needs. It helps families determine 'What do we really want out of our screens?' versus 'What do marketers convince us we want out of them?' *The Screentime Solution* is readable and doable! Rather than coasting, and then suffering harmful consequences, reading *The Screentime Solution* will gain the reader clarity over the tough decisions like when to provide a smartphone and when to allow social media. Emily has given us a developmentally grounded road map for what to do at each age, all with the understanding that parents are human, and we do like our own screens as well. Emily suggests using my favorite parenting tool—setting expectations—which can work miracles against persuasive technology. This book gives parents the right questions to ask and techniques that can be used today and as technology changes. The word of the year will be Emily Cherkin's 'tech-intentional'!"

—JEAN ROGERS, MSEd, certified parent educator and director of the Screen Time Action Network at Fairplay

"Emily Cherkin's *The Screentime Solution* is a comprehensive guide *all* parents should turn to for answers about screen time. This book goes beyond 'Too much screen time will rot your brain.' Emily helps us understand *why* making educated and wise decisions about screens and our children matters, and what we can do to combat the deluge of digital decisions coming at our families every day. Add this book to your list of parenting must-reads!"

—ANDREA DAVIS, founder of Better Screen Time and author of *Creating a Tech-Healthy Family*

"Navigating screentime in the family is complex and often painful. Emily Cherkin's *The Screentime Solution* helps map the tech-use landscape in a nonjudgmental and family values-aligned way. Cherkin gives age-specific, clear, and detailed guidance to help parents pace their kids' adoption of technology. This book isn't just for parents of tweens and teens, it is a treasure for parents of young children who have the unique opportunity to build their family's tech culture intentionally from the very start!"

—DR. TRACY MCDANIEL, ND

"In *The Screentime Solution*, expert Emily Cherkin has put together a phenomenal resource for parents. As a parent coach and child safety expert myself, I see parents continually struggle with when to let kids on screens, how much screentime is too much, how to enforce boundaries around screens, and how to create a family culture of responsible and healthy screen use. Because these are such huge challenges, I love that Emily focuses on curiosity, presence, communication, and relationships as the foundation for managing these challenging issues. I also appreciate her emphasis on skill-building and making sure that we, as parents, are not handing screens over before our children are ready. Her clear-cut, savvy advice is much needed in this day and age, and this is a volume every parent should have on their shelves."

—CHRISTY KEATING, JD, founder of The Heartful Parent Collective and host of The Safe Parenting Summit

"'We can do this' sums up this wonderful book. Emily's positive coaching tone walks parents through solutions step by step. Her warm style and practical strategies remove the shame and overwhelm of supporting children with their screentime. A perfect blend of facts and solutions— all in a quick, easy read for busy families."

—GILLIAN JARVIS, child occupational therapist at Growing Pathways

A Judgment-Free Guide to
Becoming a Tech-Intentional Family

# THE SCREENTIME SOLUTION

# EMILY CHERKIN, MEd

GREENLEAF
BOOK GROUP PRESS

Published by Greenleaf Book Group Press
Austin, Texas
www.gbgpress.com

Distributed by Greenleaf Book Group

For ordering information or special discounts for bulk purchases, please contact
Greenleaf Book Group at PO Box 91869, Austin, TX 78709, 512.891.6100.

Design and composition by Greenleaf Book Group and Mimi Bark
Cover design by Greenleaf Book Group and Mimi Bark
Cover image used under license from ©Shutterstock.com/Jomic;
©Shutterstock.com/3D Vector; ©Shutterstock.com/BadaLstudio;
©Shutterstock.com/hvostik; ©Shutterstock.com/AF studio

Publisher's Cataloging-in-Publication data is available.

Print ISBN: 979-8-88645-112-2

eBook ISBN: 979-8-88645-113-9


To offset the number of trees consumed in the printing of our books, Greenleaf
donates a portion of the proceeds from each printing to the Arbor Day
Foundation. Greenleaf Book Group has replaced over 50,000 trees since 2007.


Printed in the United States of America on acid-free paper

23  24  25  26  27  28  29  30     10  9  8  7  6  5  4  3  2  1

First Edition

This book is dedicated to childhood:
The messy, the tactile, the courageous.

And to all parents everywhere:
This *is* a fight worth having.

# CONTENTS

# INTRODUCTION

I don't actually know how to type.

—CARLY, 11 YEARS OLD

**A FEW YEARS AGO,** I worked as an academic tutor for a sixth grader named Carly.[1] Her local public school had recently moved to a one-to-one iPad program, meaning every child had their own device and there were no physical textbooks, planners, or notebooks. All school-related activities—reading, writing, note-taking, planning, and homework—would be done via apps and websites on the school-issued iPad.

Carly arrived in my office to work on a science assignment: read a chapter and answer some questions. That seemed straightforward enough. After pulling out her school-issued iPad, Carly opened a series of tabs: Google Classroom, Schoology, Notability, a few eBooks, and an internet browser. She opened a chapter in her eBook and then opened and downloaded the list of questions, which she accessed via

---

1    Names and identifying information have been changed to protect the privacy of individuals included in this book.

her teacher's class page on Schoology. Then, she uploaded the question list to Notability. "It's easier for me to write in the answers here," she explained.

At this point, she still hadn't read the chapter or the questions. I then watched as Carly continued by opening the tab with her eBook and pulling up the index to find the section she was supposed to read. She scrolled for a while but then gave up because the digital version didn't make finding pages easy. Carly then opened her Google web browser, copied and pasted the first question from the handout in Notability, and dropped it into the search bar. Without reading the search results, Carly copied and pasted the first answer that popped up directly into her Notability app.

Before she moved on to the second question, prepared to repeat the same steps, I stopped her and asked gently, "Does your teacher know that you copy and paste?"

Carly replied that her teacher didn't really know because "she doesn't read our answers."

Cautiously, I asked, "Do you know what plagiarism is?"

Carly answered, "Sort of. Usually, I edit a little of what I copy and paste into my own words, but it is way easier to do this than to retype the answer."

"It takes longer to type your own words out?"

She admitted, "Yeah, well . . . I actually don't know how to type."

Shocked by her admission, I realized how backward things had become.

## THE PROBLEM

Device use and screentime among children have increased significantly during the past two decades. My children were born in 2008 and 2011. They arrived just after Apple released the first iPhone and iPad, respectively. I use their childhoods as a metric by which to measure changes in device use. For my oldest in his toddler years, screentime was limited to a few ad-free games on our phones or *Thomas & Friends* videos; not much else existed. But by the time my second child was a toddler, preschoolers were wandering around with personal tablets, tapping away at games designed for young fingers and eyes.

An American child born after 2015 was likely raised with a computer in the house and learned to use it before kindergarten—and in a very short period, this early access to screen-based technology fundamentally shifted how we parent. Today, nearly 31% of eight-year-olds have a smartphone; by age 12, 71 % do. Teens are averaging eight or more hours per day on screen-based tech, and tweens are averaging 5.5—and these are hours *outside* of school time. Add the screentime that came with remote learning during the pandemic, and it's no surprise that the amount of time children spend in front of digital devices has risen: although technology existed in classrooms pre-COVID, children's use of screen-based media increased by 17% in just two years.[2] The pandemic further changed how we learn, teach, and parent, adding fuel to an already-growing fire.

Although scientists and educators have long expressed concerns about the impacts of screen-based technology on children's health and brain development, the reality is that we simply do not have the long-term data yet to know how much is really too much. But we *do* have decades of research that tells us what children need to grow and thrive—and none of that research points to screen-based technology as the best path forward.

---

2    Victoria Rideout, MA; Alanna Peebles, PhD; Supreet Mann, PhD; and Michael B. Robb, PhD, "Common Sense Census: Media Use by Tweens and Teens," Common Sense Media, 2021, https://www.commonsensemedia.org/sites/default/files/research/report/8-18-census-integrated-report-final-web_0.pdf.

Smartphones and tablets were not designed for children. Social media companies continue to push platforms they know are harmful to young people, and parents are caught in the middle. Overwhelmed by the mental demands of busy modern lives, we all use technology as a tool to help us organize, manage, plan, work, and communicate. Just as often, we use it to distract, entertain, or socialize—and our children use screen-based technology in many of the same ways. Screens have become part of the daily fabric of our lives.

Through my work with parents, schools, and professional organizations, I increasingly hear stories that illustrate how common—and complex—these changes are for families and children. Families everywhere struggle to find balance with screentime. These are some of the questions I hear the most: How much is too much? At what age should we give our child a smartphone? How do we teach them about safety and privacy? How do we monitor it all?

## THE CONSEQUENCES

The concern is not occasional screen use; it is *excessive* screen use. However, giving a definitive answer to "How much is too much screentime?" can be challenging because it might be different from one child to the next. And the impacts of excessive screen use vary greatly, so how it affects children is worth a closer look.

I define excessive screen use as any type, amount, or duration of screen-based technology that interferes with, impacts, or displaces healthy developmental activities and interests. For example, one 2018 study revealed that even moderate use of screens ("only" four hours per day) was associated with less curiosity, lower self-control, and increased distractibility.[3] Instead of expressing their creativity on

---

3    Jean M. Twenge and W. Keith Campbell, "Associations between Screen Time and Lower Psychological Well-Being among Children and Adolescents: Evidence from a Population-Based Study," Preventive Medicine Reports 12 (December 2018): 271–83.

devices, young people prefer watching videos; according to a 2019 Common Sense Media Census, the "vast majority" of young people do not enjoy making their own content. And because of excessive screen use, only 35% of teens say they read for pleasure every day; another 21% say that happens less than once a month or never.[4] Interestingly, from 1998 through 2007, the publication of the Harry Potter series had children lining up outside of bookstores, a new generation of readers eager to devour hardcovers and paperbacks for pleasure. What is today's equivalent?

Even beyond decreasing attention spans, creativity, and reading for pleasure, excessive screen use has affected children's basic needs. If a teen is spending seven or more hours a day outside of school and homework on screens, what time is left for eating, sleeping, exercising, socializing, and family time?

To be clear, not all screen use is necessarily bad. But the challenge for today's parents, especially those of my own generation, is to try to separate the good from the not-so-good while also seeking to help our children—and ourselves—find balance.

## THE COMPLEXITIES OF PARENTING IN THE DIGITAL AGE

The goal of this book is to provide a map for parents to understand the challenges of excessive screen use, why they are happening, and, most importantly, what we can do about them. Lurking over our shoulders throughout all of this, however, are the technology companies that love to push the burden of managing screentime solely onto parents without making actual product design decisions that take to heart the best interests of children. It's easier to make this the

---

4    Victoria Rideout, MA and Michael B. Robb, PhD, "The Common Sense Census: Media Use by Tweens and Teens," Common Sense Media, 2019, https://www.commonsensemedia.org/sites/default/files/research/report/2019-census-8-to-18-key-findings-updated.pdf.

responsibility of parents than for tech companies to make business changes that might negatively impact their bottom line.

I'm not here to demonize the technology industry. Full disclosure: I'm married to someone who works in that very field, and I make no secret of it. Change can and should come from all sides, and you can be sure that we talk about these issues a lot in our house. So while I'm not here to point fingers, I do firmly believe that the technology industry needs to be part of the solution. When tech executives send their own children to nature-based school programs with no-screens policies, we know there is something *they* know about excessive tech use that we do not. And we should take note.

The apps we and our children use are designed to hook and hold our attention. In a 2018 *Psychology Today* article, Bill Fulton, an expert in user experience research, strategy, and design with graduate-level training in social psychology, says tellingly, "If game designers are going to pull a person away from every other voluntary social activity or hobby or pastime, they're going to have to engage that person at a very deep level in every possible way they can."[5] The same applies to social media, online video, and other digital products. So, as I tell parents all the time, this *really* isn't a fair fight. Once we know this and understand why, then we can start to make intentional choices about how we use screen-based technology in our homes.

Numerous well-researched studies highlight the negative impacts of excessive screen use on children's physical, mental, and social health; learning; and emotional well-being. However, most parents don't read complex research studies. Moreover, they feel confused about the conflicting information they hear (especially that funded by the technology industry itself), and they're often uncertain about the

---

5    Richard Freed, "How the Tech Industry Uses Psychology to Hook Children," *Psychology Today*, October 24, 2018.

safety risks of so much time online. While most parents are concerned about the headline-grabbing stories of pornography, cyberbullying, and exploitation, many are unaware of the deeply problematic issues around data and privacy—and the massive amounts of money technology companies reap from the widely available data about our children and their online behavior. Data mining doesn't make for flashy headlines, but the risks are real and serious.

How have we gotten to a point where it is considered normal for a teenager to spend seven or more hours a day on a screen *outside* of schoolwork? How are we collectively comfortable with handing phones to nine-year-olds because "everyone else has them"? (They don't.) How can we be so in the dark about what data is being collected about our children?

Parents, these challenges are *not* our fault. But it *is* our responsibility to be more than monitors. We must be mentors, role models, and teachers. We must ask tough questions of our schools and push back on Big Tech's claim that this is a parenting problem.

And we all want to do better; we're just not sure what to do or where to start. That's why I am so glad you're reading this book. *I firmly believe that by understanding the complexities of this issue and setting healthy boundaries, we will be better equipped to fight for our children's future cognitive, mental, and emotional health.*

## THE SOLUTION: BECOMING TECH-INTENTIONAL

I always tell parents, "I am not anti-tech. I am tech-intentional." It's a term I coined and trademarked, and this is how I define it:

> Being tech-intentional means using screen-based technologies that enhance, nurture, and support ourselves, our children, and our families in ways that align with

our values, and resisting, delaying, or limiting any type
of screen use that interferes with our healthy mental,
physical, cognitive, and emotional development.

This book is about becoming tech-intentional parents who raise tech-intentional children. *The Screentime Solution* provides you with research-supported, developmentally appropriate tools and serves as a nonjudgmental guide to finding balance with screentime in your family. It is written by me: a parent, former teacher, and consultant who lives and breathes these very struggles. It's the book I wish I had had when my children were young but needed so much more when they became tweens.

I hope that these new tools will empower you to make meaningful, tech-intentional changes that benefit the whole family. But like any parenting book, some of these chapters will resonate more than others. That's okay. This approach, much like parenting, is not one size fits all. Children from the same households will respond differently to different content, different amounts of time online, and different limits. It will take nuance, effort, courage, and discomfort to build new habits and achieve the right balance. Use the tools that work best for you. And for quick and easy reference tools, at the end of each chapter, I've included a TL;DR ("too long; didn't read") section, which summarizes the takeaways.

Conversely, after reading this book, you may want to change all the screentime rules in your home. Even if you feel sorely tempted, do not change all your rules at once. It won't work. It's best to implement the strategies that best fit your family's specific needs and circumstances.

If you're looking for more resources, including the websites of thought leaders and organizations, books, articles, and other research that I find useful, please visit my website at thescreentimeconsultant.com. I am constantly collecting information on screen use, and I frequently update my "Resources" page.

In my own journey as a teacher and parent, I have struggled, failed, and tried again to figure out what works and what doesn't. I don't always get it right. But the more I talk to other parents and face these challenges myself, the more I have come to believe that we can do hard things—and that doing these hard things matters for our children.

It *is* possible to serve as healthy technology role models and raise our children in a way that aligns with our values, even in a world that grows more technological by the day.

We can do this. Let's get started.

# CHAPTER 1

# NOPE, IT'S NOT LIKE WHEN WE WERE KIDS

The world is more addictive than it was 40 years ago. And . . . the world will get more addictive in the next 40 years than it did in the last 40. . . . We'll increasingly be defined by what we say no to.

—PAUL GRAHAM, FOUNDER OF Y COMBINATOR

For the first time as a parent, I feel completely incapacitated when it comes to my youngest and her phone. And I've raised eight children.

—A PARENT

**MANY PARENTS HAVE APPROACHED** me to say, sometimes defensively, "*I* watched television and played video games as a kid, and *I* turned out fine."

Perhaps. But the television and video games of our childhood were nothing like the streaming shows and video games available to our children today.

My generation, the latter part of Gen X, was born into a world that did not know the internet, but we are raising our children in a generation that will never know a world without it. We had friends with pagers, not smartphones. Playing with friends meant Monopoly or hide-and-seek, not Minecraft or posting on social media. Today's parents are truly a bridge between the analog and the digital.

When I give presentations to parents, I start by asking my audiences to fill in a blank: "When I was a child, technology meant . . ." My fellow Gen X and older Millennial parenting peers offer up examples like early Macintosh computers, the Oregon Trail game, graphing calculators, pagers, CD-ROMs, electronic typewriters, floppy disks, dusty computer labs at school, and cordless phones. I put up a slide with images of these clunky old machines, many rendered useless (or deemed iconic) today. Several people chuckle.

Then, I ask, "For your child, what does technology mean?" Now, the answers rolling in are brand names, social media sites, gaming platforms, and high-end digital devices. On my slide, brightly colored icons—logos that are recognizable to adults and children alike—dot the page. In fact, when my own daughter first saw the slide, she named nearly every icon correctly despite never having used many of the products herself. By contrast, when she had seen the old-school slide projector on my Gen X slide, she asked, "What is that?"

There is no question that our childhood experiences differ dramatically from those of our children. The following demonstrates the significant differences we've seen in screen use between just Gen X and Gen Z, which are separated by only a single generation. But we've seen and will continue to see similarly drastic changes in tech use between, for example, Millennials and Gen Alpha or between Gen Z and those born after 2025.

## A TYPICAL WEEKDAY FOR GEN XERS

Many children in the 1980s were latchkey kids: we wore house keys on a string around our necks, came home to an empty house, and fended for ourselves in the after-school hours. If we didn't go to an on-site program, after-school specials on TV provided entertainment until one or both of our working parents got home. The neighborhood soccer team might organize a weekly practice or two, but more commonly, when the weather was nice, we would round up other kids in the neighborhood to play outside, ride bikes, and create our own fun. Our parents might keep tabs on us, but we also knew our neighbors were looking out for us, and we knew to be home by dark.

School was the place we could get a break from our parents, who rarely communicated with our teachers. We not only learned basic academics but got to play during several recesses each day. Playing games or learning on computers was limited to computer lab in elementary school or elective computer courses in middle or high school.

## A TYPICAL WEEKDAY FOR GEN ZERS

Today's children spend more time around their parents physically but engage with them less emotionally. After-school activities now crowd afternoon schedules, and it is not uncommon to find one child participating in multiple extracurricular events each day of the week, often at a significant expense to the parents. Neighborhood soccer has been replaced by elite club soccer teams whose membership fees run into the thousands. There is little downtime for children in the afternoons as harried parents try to juggle work schedules with parenting, which means driving all over town to get children to their activities.

After-school specials on television don't exist because video streaming services allow infinite choices on a plethora of platforms at any hour of the day. Kids who have time to watch shows usually do it on the go, such as on a parent's phone or a personal tablet in the car.

Today, parents do not leave children home alone until they are at least in middle school because the news headlines, which we receive in regular doses via notifications on our phones throughout the day, remind us constantly of the risks in the real world. Free play with neighborhood kids might happen on a weekend, when it isn't crowded out by obligatory birthday parties, scheduled playdates, and more extracurriculars. Downtime is a rare commodity.

Meanwhile, during the school day, increased standardized testing to meet national requirements means less time for recess, which, along with the arts, has shrunk in priority and duration over the years. And while computer lab might remain a weekly event for some elementary school students, the creep of technology into the classroom, especially in middle and high school, steadily increased in the 2010s, in part funded by technology companies seeking early brand loyalty but also on the wave of the so-called 21st-century skills movement, which deemed that certain technological skills were innovative and therefore imperative to future success.

## HOMEWORK FOR GEN XERS

Homework looked very different in the 1980s. In elementary school, we had weekly spelling word lists to study or the occasional science fair project (volcanos, anyone?) to complete. In middle and high school, we had math problems to work on from a heavy textbook we would lug back and forth between home and school. We wrote out essays by hand on paper for first drafts, maybe typed out the next draft on a word processor, and saved it on a floppy disk for printing. If we forgot our homework (or claimed our dog ate it), teachers asked us to bring it the following day or stay in at lunch to complete it.

## HOMEWORK FOR GEN ZERS

Research continually shows the benefits of reading as the most useful form of homework, whereas busy work, worksheets, online reading, and other time wasters contribute little to student knowledge or critical thinking. Yet these are common in the homework experience of a child in the 2010s and 2020s. Elementary school homework comes in the form of weekly homework packets, created perhaps to meet the demands of highly anxious parents who want their kids to always be learning but also in response to meeting standardized testing requirements, which redirect resources to core subject class work and homework and away from the arts, the library, and recess. More recently, homework, even in elementary, is now located, completed, and turned in via online learning management platforms.

## PARENT–TEACHER COMMUNICATIONS FOR GEN XERS

Rarely did our teachers communicate directly with our parents outside of back-to-school night events. If a note got sent home, it was related to serious behavioral infractions, not missing vocabulary homework, and most parents and kids considered a note home a pretty big deal. Generally speaking, teachers communicated directly with students and reached out to parents only when they absolutely needed to.

## PARENT–TEACHER COMMUNICATIONS FOR GEN ZERS

Far from hands-off, parents today are heavily involved in children's school lives, checking progress on a school's website or grading platform, emailing the teacher regularly, and, when they have the time in between work meetings, volunteering as classroom readers and room parents. They communicate frequently with their children's teachers via email, school websites, or other digital platforms. Online grade books, intended to proactively provide us with easy updates on our children's in-class progress, instead became huge sources of anxiety and further justification to contact a teacher. A child has little incentive to ask their teacher for an explanation about a lower-than-desired grade when they know their mom will just email to ask.

In my own teaching career, I could tell that parents were refreshing their browsers to constantly update their child's grades. If I didn't immediately score an assignment, parents would email to ask about the delay. When I did grade it, they would email to ask why it wasn't an *A*. When I explained that grades were only one measure of performance and that my students always had an opportunity to redo an assignment, the parents wanted to know what specifically their child needed to do. Sadly, this parental overinvolvement triangulated the teacher–student relationship, and the critically important skill-building experiences that students needed to practice during their school years were hijacked by anxious parents.

## WATCHING TV FOR GEN XERS

Regardless of how much time we spent in front of a screen back in the 1980s or '90s, there were only so many choices about what we could watch and when. It wasn't at all the same as it is today. Many of us grew up with just a handful of channels, and to change them, we had to physically stand up and turn a knob. If we wanted to watch something different, we would try to time our channel surfing during commercial breaks so we wouldn't miss any content of the original show in case we decided to go back.

As children in the 1980s, we also had to learn to plan our week around the shows we wanted to watch and when they aired. My parents limited a lot of our television viewing, though I have fond memories of coming home from elementary school and getting to watch *Sesame Street* while I ate my after-school snack of apple slices, cheddar cheese, and crackers. Sometimes, we were allowed to watch cartoons on the weekends when they aired, but my favorite TV viewing time was the Thursday night lineup. I always looked forward to the coming week's episodes. There were times, however, when nothing good was on TV, and if we complained about it to our parents, they shrugged and sent us outside to play. Even on days when we stayed home sick from school, our television-viewing options were limited primarily to boring soap operas, game shows, or talk shows. Yawn.

*How* we watch television has also changed significantly. During our childhoods, it was a rare kid who had a personal television set in their bedroom. TV sets were usually located in a living or family room, we may have only owned one or two sets, and we had to share them with other people—most often our siblings. Even if we didn't realize it at the time, watching TV was an opportunity to work on our relationships. How many of us remember fighting with a sibling or parent for control of the remote?

While our parents might not look back fondly on those fights, the truth is that they provided great skill-building for us as kids. We were learning not only that other people have differing opinions from our own but also that we might have to negotiate, compromise, and share or else our parents would shut off the television altogether. Our common end goal of being entertained meant we had to work it out.

If we traveled as children in the 1980s, our parents had to find ways to occupy us for several seat-bound hours, especially if the one movie playing on a flight wasn't kid friendly. Long car trips were lessons in boredom and occupying our time with group games, such as finding license plates from different states or counting telephone poles as they flashed by. If we listened to music, we had to take turns picking the cassette tapes or radio stations, which provided more chances to practice our social and negotiation skills.

## WATCHING TV FOR GEN ZERS

The entire concept of watching television in the 2010s and 2020s is completely unlike that of the 1980s. Most of our children today expect that whatever show they want to watch is available immediately, on any device, in any location.

Until I became a parent, I did not think about how unique an experience my weekly Thursday night viewings would be compared with my own children's experience of television years later. Once, when my children were still young, we stayed in a hotel room while on vacation. It was a surreal experience to try to explain to my five-year-old that he could not just watch *Thomas & Friends* on this particular TV even though, in his mind, this screen was exactly like the one at home, on which we sometimes played his *Thomas & Friends* DVDs. He didn't understand why we could provide that for him at home but not at the hotel.

With the increase of mobile tech use, children now watch television—or rather, content—in line at the grocery store or while waiting for a sibling's soccer practice to finish. And for our children, streaming content on multiple platforms today means unlimited options if we have Wi-Fi, and in the rare situation that we don't have Wi-Fi, they can view pre-downloaded shows.

This instant gratification is very different from the delayed gratification we had to practice over the course of a whole week to watch the next 30-minute episode of a favorite show in the 1980s. Today, there is never a moment when children say, "There's nothing good to watch" because there is never a shortage of available—if questionable—content.

We have dramatically changed the shared experience that used to be watching TV. Even if we fought over the remote or what show to watch, we were building conflict-resolution skills in the process. Today, we hand separate iPads to our kids in the interest of preventing conflict without realizing that resolving conflict facilitates growth and learning.

## THE DISPLACEMENT HYPOTHESIS

Beyond anecdotal comparisons (Appendix A provides a point-by-point contrast of yesterday's and today's technology and a commentary about what might have been lost in the transition), research shows that how we experience childhood has changed drastically across generations. For example, the work of Douglas Gentile, an award-winning psychologist, author, and educator who runs the Media Research Lab at Iowa State University, reveals that in the 1950s, the average American child spent about 68 hours per week participating in sports, playing with friends, reading books, exploring the outdoors, or practicing a musical instrument. By 2010, that number had dropped to 14 hours per week—a nearly 80% decrease. Even more concerning, meaningful one-on-one engagement with parents had decreased by the first decade of the millennium: outside of normal family life interactions, mothers were spending on average only 2.5 hours—and fathers a paltry 30 minutes—per week connecting with their children. Yet children were spending 51 hours a week using the computer for non-school-related activities, playing video games, or watching TV.

Gentile refers to this shift as *the displacement effect*: the more time we spend on screens, the less time we spend doing some other activity, such as engaging in hobbies and interests. Modern-day children have not only displaced their "free" time with extra screentime, but their parents are spending less time engaging with their children, who in turn spend more time on screens. Gentile's research makes obvious the importance of setting limits on children's screentime—if not our own. But convincing parents that screentime consumption today is different from our own childhoods is sometimes tricky.[6]

## THE COVID-19 PANDEMIC: ADDING FUEL TO THE FIRE

Since our childhoods in the 1970s and '80s, major cultural changes have shaped and continue to shape family life in terms of our relationship with screens and technology. First came the launch of America Online (more commonly known as AOL) in 1983 and the popularization of the World Wide Web in the '90s. Then, mobile tech began to proliferate in the 2000s, with the arrival of the iPhone in 2007 dramatically changing the way we made phone calls, checked email, organized our schedules, listened to music, watched videos, shopped, took photographs, and connected socially. But when the pandemic arrived in late 2019 and spread rapidly throughout 2020, we were forced not only to change our routines and behavior in the name of public health and safety but also to adapt how we work, parent, and support our children's learning. Tech use rose significantly, with screentime for school piled onto screentime for entertainment, and the effects will inevitably be far-reaching.

---

6    Douglas A. Gentile, Rachel A. Reimer, Amy I. Nathanson, David A. Walsh, and Joey C. Eisenmann, "Protective Effects of Parental Monitoring of Children's Media Use: A Prospective Study," National Library of Medicine, Multicenter Study, *JAMA Pediatrics*, May 2014, 168(5):479-84. doi: 10.1001/jamapediatrics.2014.146, https://pubmed.ncbi.nlm.nih.gov/24686493/.

COVID-19 didn't create the screentime problems we are facing today; it just added fuel to the already-burning fire. In terms of physical impacts, rates of myopia (permanent near-sightedness) were already high before COVID, but researchers believe excessive screen use during the pandemic accelerated vision problems in children. Children also gained and lost weight because of the decreased exercise and increased stress brought on by excessive screen use. Meanwhile, mental health issues, such as anxiety and depression, continue to rise. A generation ago, pediatricians treated mostly physical problems in children, such as disease and broken bones. Today, pediatricians report that most of their patients' complaints are about mental and emotional issues, such as anxiety, self-harm, eating disorders, and depression.

Beyond the physical and mental consequences of excessive tech use during the pandemic are behavioral concerns. After more than a year of remote learning and virtual socializing, screentime battles remain a central source of tension for families. Young children have struggled to filter and discern what is useful from what is distracting. Older children and teens are experiencing high rates of mental illness. Additionally, the more time children spend online for learning or entertainment, the greater the potential to be taken advantage of by those who seek to do harm. Indeed, cases of online child exploitation rose by nearly three million in a single year, increasing to more than 4.2 million reports to the National Center for Missing and Exploited Children in April 2020.

Exhausted by the impacts of a global pandemic, parents remain overwhelmed and confused about how to set and enforce limits on screentime. They look for apps and monitoring software to help but then come to me with stories of how their children find workarounds. Parents use screentime to incentivize and motivate, but children seem unmoved. After all, homework and planners are on learning management systems, grades appear in online grade books, and apps and platforms are as easy to collect as Pokémon cards. COVID-19 only exacerbated the concerns about excessive tech use that have been growing since the introduction of AOL and the iPhone in decades past.

## DISPROPORTIONATE HARMS

COVID-19 impacted different populations differently; screentime does as well. For many families across demographics, the pandemic drove screen use even higher as remote learning and quarantine decreased opportunities to socialize and connect with peers in person. Unfortunately, the increased use of screens also disproportionately affected young people in lower socioeconomic groups. According to Common Sense Media, tweens from higher-income homes use almost three hours less of screen media per day than those from lower-income households. Teens in higher-income families averaged seven hours and 16 minutes per day on screen-based entertainment compared with more than nine hours per day for lower- and middle-income children. As research continues to demonstrate that excessive screen use can have negative impacts on learning and brain development, this inequity is indeed worrisome.

There is a paradox in that the very communities that are most susceptible to COVID-19 infections—and who are therefore more inclined to stick with remote learning longer to protect their health—are also the communities most negatively impacted by excessive screen use. This merging of crises exacerbated and will continue to exacerbate the inequities that exist in our country. Knowing this, the fight for our children's future cognitive and emotional health is even more important. We can't turn back the clock, but we can change the course of the future by how we choose to parent our children around screen use—and how we continue to advocate for *all* children.

## TECH-BASED VERSUS TRADITIONAL PLAY

Any new technology causes some hand-wringing. When high-speed trains first came out, for example, people worried about passengers getting brain damage from watching the rapidly passing scenery. That sounds absurd now, but some pushback about new technologies is normal and even necessary: we *should* speculate about the benefits and risks of any new technology. Even as I write this, ChatGPT, an AI predictive language tool, is in its infancy but has the potential to forever change how we read, research, and write. And when it comes to children, we must look critically at the impact of these new tech-based tools on brain development.

Jenny Radesky, a developmental–behavioral pediatrician and assistant professor of pediatrics at the University of Michigan, has documented multiple ways that classic forms of play from our childhoods (e.g., with LEGO and other blocks) differ from the tech-based play of our children's childhoods (e.g., with iPad games and apps). For example, app designers control the play in digital games, whereas children develop autonomy and are in control in unstructured play. The habit of using digital entertainment to keep kids busy or quiet also decreases parent–child interaction and inhibits children's ability to learn to self-regulate their emotions.

Furthermore, whereas digital games grab our children's attention, unstructured play builds attention, which has dramatic effects on our children's focusing skills—and it is fascinating to note that rates of attention deficit hyperactivity disorder have risen in the past 20 years of increasing screen use. The rewards of each kind of play also differ: apps and games provide many external rewards (e.g., points, tokens, or coins), but the rewards of traditional play are internal and social and have lasting benefits as children learn to struggle and problem-solve, which are vital skills for adulthood.

The social interactivity of games has also changed immensely over the decades. Most apps and games today are designed for solitary play. They do not invite others to join in the way traditional play does. Social, in-person play allows for shared experiences, which builds social and emotional skills. As MIT professor and author Sherry Turkle puts it, we are "alone together" in our consumption of screens—similarly, our children are becoming more isolated in these new forms of play.

## THE BENEFITS OF BOREDOM

Although there are many other ways in which our childhoods differ from modern-day childhoods, perhaps the biggest shift, outside of increased internet and device access, is simply the overwhelming number of choices available. There is no shortage of shows to watch, games to play, and social media feeds to scroll through.

During our childhoods, when we told our parents, "I'm bored," they responded with "Go outside" or "Go read a book." When our children today say, "I'm bored," often they mean "I want screentime" or "I don't know how to entertain myself because I've spent so much time on screens, I'm out of practice on how to play alone." And children today don't say, "There's nothing to watch" because the content made for kids is available 24/7.

Nowadays, boredom gets a bad rap. We see it as something that needs to be fixed. But here's the truth: boredom is the birthplace of creativity. When we embrace our restlessness and tedium, we come up with our best ideas. Children are naturally imaginative and curious. A bored child who is allowed to wander, explore, and problem-solve is going to invent some wonderful stuff.

As parents in this digital age, we might look back on our own childhood experiences and remember distinctive, even painful, moments of boredom. However, we can also likely connect that boredom to inspired bursts of creativity and imagination, which led us to try new things or test new ideas in ways we never expected. Today, while apps and streamed content might *show* us new and innovative ways to do things, they do the work for us; in fact, those programs may even stem from someone else's creativity-inspiring boredom. Our job is to recognize that boredom is not a problem in need of fixing, and we must seek out alternatives to a screen in our attempts to "solve" it.

## THE CHALLENGES OF ACCELERATING CHANGE

Even beyond interrupting boredom, we might be aware of our tendency to hand over devices in the name of fixing other short-term issues, such as stopping a tantrum or incentivizing behavior. But as educator and writer Alfie Kohn says, "The best that carrots—or sticks—can do is change people's behavior temporarily. They can never create a lasting commitment to an action or a value, and often they have exactly the opposite effect."[7] Parents today want to do better by their children, but no precedent has been set. We are the tip of the spear in defining what it means to be parents in the digital age, and it can be hard to keep up.

The need to stay on top of technology has changed drastically, not just since our childhoods but even more so in just a decade. As parents, we barely have time to adapt to one technological marvel before the next one is released. We accept each new iteration of the iPhone as they come out (there have been 38 versions so far if you're counting). And with every new technological innovation comes the fear of something else being lost. When steam trains started running during the 1850s and 1860s, technophobes worried that the rapid acceleration would cause a form of anxiety and aggression called "railway

---

7    Alfie Kohn, "Rewards Are Still Bad News (25 Years Later)" *New York Times*, October 28, 2018, https://www.alfiekohn.org/article/rewards-25-years-later.

madness" and women's uteruses to fall out. When MTV launched in 1981, its first music video was the aptly named and soon-to-be-iconic "Video Killed the Radio Star" by The Buggles. And although the humble pay phone reached its peak of 2.7 million across the United States in the mid-1990s, by 2018, only 100,000 phone booths remained—a casualty of more than 96% of Americans owning a cell phone and 81% a smartphone (according to that year's *Mobile Fact Sheet* from the Pew Research Center). The pace at which these innovations and corresponding losses occur has only accelerated since the 1980s.

The sheer number of devices that now occupy our households has also increased. Today, most of us have at least one personal device, such as a smartphone, but we also have laptops, desktop computers, tablets, and other devices that allow us access to content 24/7. We accept that email, social media, and online news sites are just "the way we do things now." Even as platforms rapidly proliferate and evolve, we adapt our social, personal, and work lives to accommodate these technological shifts.

Given all this, it shouldn't have come as a surprise to me as a parent when my son's first lesson in kindergarten was technology based, but it did. One day, a piece of yellow paper in his take-home folder told us that Max needed to learn how to invoke the Control-Alt-Delete command on a keyboard. The teacher explained that these "new young techies" would need to be able to press the three keys at once, enter a username, and enter a password using an underscore. This assignment was not just to help the students participate in their weekly computer lab classes, which we were excited for Max to participate in; it was also for the students to log on to the district computers to take standardized tests. We weren't prepared for this. We thought we had done our due diligence by monitoring how many *Thomas & Friends* DVDs we allowed him to watch at home and limiting the amount of swiping he did on our iPhones!

Ten days into kindergarten, our son did not know how to read or write much more than his own name but needed to learn how to log on to a computer to take a standardized test, the questions on which he would not even be able to read. It had not occurred to me that Max's kindergarten experience in 2013 would differ so much from my own in 1983. Nor did I realize that after 2013, things would only further change, with more and more EdTech surfacing in the classroom. And I couldn't possibly have predicted that in 2020, most students around the United States would be learning remotely during a pandemic. New technologies always influence culture, but I was astonished at the exponential impact that new screen- and internet-based technologies were having on childhood, education, and parenting.

## THE IMPACTS OF SCREEN-BASED TECHNOLOGY

Although scientists and educators have expressed increasing concerns about the long-term impacts of so much screen-based technology on children's health and brain development, the reality is that we simply do not have the long-term data yet to know how much is too much. However, there are enough red flags for us to sit up and pay attention. And it's hard not to feel like managing screentime is yet another thing we need to download an app for (oh, the irony!).

So for parents who feel behind, uncertain, and overwhelmed, you are not alone. Many parents who reach out to me for support have stories of the tween who finds ways around their carefully established parental controls, the fifth grader without a device who feels left out because their friends all communicate via text, the teen who can't get off their phone, and the video gamer who has stopped attending class or doing homework. They will say, "It wasn't like this for me when I was a kid—I didn't have this much access! We didn't have social media! All their friends have phones! What are we supposed to do?"

Despite these struggles, we as parents have strong opinions about screentime, especially when it comes to our own children. We are reluctant to wade too deep into advocating for more restrictions because we realize that limiting screens may inconvenience our own lives or negatively impact our children's friendships. But consuming too much screentime impacts our relationships, skill development, and mental and emotional health. As parents, we cannot take our own childhood experiences with screens as gospel for what we do with our children today.

In contrast to the worries and anxieties about screentime, I hear all the time that tech-based tools have "taught my preschooler to read" or "inspired my eight-year-old to code their own app." One parent argued that building with blocks in a game like Minecraft is no different from building with blocks in real life. Indeed, not all screen-based technologies are bad. Some apps can and do teach skills or provide inspiration. One could argue that watching *Sesame Street* on TV in our childhood taught my generation the letters of the alphabet. But for those of us who did not grow up with a wide range of algorithm-driven, screen-based games and social media, we must understand how fundamentally different these platforms are from the tools of our childhood and learn about how these newer technologies impact brain growth and development differently.

## THE EVOLUTION OF SCHOOL-BASED TECHNOLOGY

My elementary school computer lab days consisted of moving the "turtle" (a cursor that I remember as a flashing green triangle), learning how to type (still an important skill), and playing endless games of Oregon Trail (where I learned the vocabulary words *meager* and *grueling*). But today, technology is far more integrated than our one-room computer labs of the 1980s and 1990s. Now, computers appear in classrooms on laptop carts or in one-to-one (i.e., one device per student) programs. Moreover, for years now, faculty professional development has extolled the benefits of tech-based tools for teaching and learning, and many school boards and administrators around the country feel that technology is the best path to future success for students, so EdTech products and platforms now proliferate in classrooms and homework.

The challenge of this school-based tech is not just that it's seemingly everywhere; it's that its effectiveness is often questionable at best. School districts have invested heavily in EdTech to supposedly bring schools into the 21st century and get curricula "in alignment" with federal standards, but that alignment is for standardized tests, the purpose of which is to questionably assess skills that are rarely of use later in life. EdTech can also dampen students' curiosity and engagement: my own district spent nine million dollars to implement a technology-based science curriculum, and I still hear from parents, teachers, and students about how much kids have lost their love of science learning because of the inane, repetitive lessons that strike children as "babyish." Similarly, some of the most popular learning-based management systems boast millions of users in thousands of schools around the world, but teachers and parents often find these platforms frustrating to use—and rarely do their benefits outweigh the displacement of other skills.

Additionally, EdTech platforms, whether educational apps or learning management systems, problematically collect a lot of personal information about students, often without parental consent or knowledge. This topic is deserving of its own book—and indeed will likely fill many in the future. Much of my advocacy work is around issues of student data privacy. We are only seeing the tip of a very large iceberg, and the long-term repercussions will be significant.

When the pandemic hit, the need for digital access to remote learning only accelerated district technology goals and seemed to justify the further expense of investing in more EdTech. Device, broadband, and Wi-Fi distribution became a top priority. Although this was indeed important for equitable access to learning in the spring of 2020, inequities deepened. Many students could only access Wi-Fi via the parking lots of schools or libraries, and many districts provided low-quality devices to students to save money—devices that often failed. Meanwhile, students whose families had the resources to purchase better-quality laptops did so. When it was first introduced a few decades ago, the focus on technology for classroom use was to close the "digital divide" and give students whose families could not afford computers equitable access to new tools. Unfortunately, the new digital divide is no longer about providing access to the devices themselves but rather about the quality, safety, and amount of time spent on the devices, and, yet again, it is children from lower socio-economic groups who are most negatively impacted.

Gen Xers didn't grow up with the World Wide Web; many of us learned of its existence only in high school, and we didn't start emailing or going online until after graduation. Flash forward 20-plus years, and the mass proliferation of EdTech and other school-provided devices during the pandemic gave our children unsupervised access to the internet, in spite of our (or our school's) attempts to filter or limit content. The internet, social media, and gaming became their playground—one much more dangerous than the schoolyards we used to play in.

Our children view a laptop or iPad provided by their school as a toy, not a learning tool. Before COVID, our children were already spending increased amounts of time on screens for entertainment and socialization—far more time than we used to spend in front of TVs in the '80s. The pandemic, quarantines, and our need to juggle work with parenting and monitoring at-home schooling only drove those hours up. Then, left to their devices (pun intended) throughout the school day, our children grew accustomed to increased time on screens for learning, and we, their exhausted parents, could only dread the fights about turning it off.

We cannot change what happened during the early days of the pandemic. But the experience of learning remotely permanently impacted both our children's educational lives and how schools "do" school. Some of it was good; some children thrived under the remote-learning conditions and may continue to learn from home using digital tools. Some families became more involved in their child's educational experience. Some parents, concerned about what they observed during remote learning, became activists advocating for decreased use of screens in the classroom or for homework. However, the fact remains that although we simply do not have long-term data to guide us on what is truly best when it comes to our children's increased screen use, we *do* have enough historically sound research on what they need to learn and develop optimally. There are enough valid concerns to slow the avalanche of EdTech and prioritize our kids' true educational and developmental needs.

## NAVIGATING TODAY'S TECH LANDSCAPE

It is rather astonishing to think about what we are doing when we hand our kids smartphones. The technology available in a modern smartphone is more sophisticated than the computers NASA used to put a man on the moon in 1969. Yet the age at which children receive their first smartphone is dropping: some estimates say the current average age is 10 years old. Now, the power of the entire internet is at the fingertips of children who may not yet know how to ride a bike or tie their own shoes.

For a parent today, it can be hard to relate to the technological world our children seem to inhabit. From the moment our parenting journey begins, we are bombarded with recommendations for tech-based products that claim to make us better parents. We are told that toddlers can learn to read using an app, that educational programming is beneficial for preschoolers, or that an iPad program in elementary school will build the skills they need to succeed. Our tweens insist that "everyone gets a smartphone" for middle school, and our teens' lives revolve around social media and gaming. Meanwhile, current technology changes by the day if not the hour, so we constantly scramble to play catch-up. Then, the clever marketing machines of technology companies continually remind us that without such exceptional tools, we simply cannot and will not be effective parents.

Parenting in the digital age is overwhelming, and rarely do we end up feeling empowered, confident, and capable. Not only do we feel like worse parents when it comes to managing screentime, but we also feel bad about our lives in general as we compare our vacations to our friends' vacations on social media, our bodies to those of models or athletes, and our children to photoshopped montages. Sure, back in the 1980s, we might have compared our physiques to models in fashion or fitness magazines or felt jealous of a friend's tropical spring break photos, but the scope of our comparison was limited to the paper we held in our hands, not the endless and polished imagery we could scroll through 24/7 on our devices.

To tackle the problem of excessive screen use among our children, parents must understand how dramatically the technological landscape has changed since our childhoods. We are the last parenting generation who will remember a childhood devoid of the internet while being the first generation of parents to navigate the concepts of screentime, social media, or remote learning. We are the only generation who will know what it is like to straddle the worlds that existed BI and AI: Before the Internet and After the Internet (and oh, the irony of those initials also standing for Artificial Intelligence).

But knowledge is power. Once we accept that things have changed and comprehend *how* they have changed since our childhoods, we can start to make choices now as parents that will impact our children's experiences and set them up for success.

## TL;DR

- Gen X childhoods are not at all like Gen Z childhoods.

- We don't have long-term data about the risks and harms of excessive screen use.

- Tech-based play is not the same as in-real-life play.

- Boredom is the birthplace of creativity.

- Knowing how technology has changed will help us make better choices for our children's screentime.

# CHAPTER 2

# SCARY VERSUS DANGEROUS: ADDRESSING ANXIETY AND SAFETY IN THE DIGITAL AGE

A child who thinks he can't do anything
on his own eventually can't.

—LENORE SKENAZY[8]

In order to grow, you must be able to let go.

—RICHARD BRANSON

**MARIA FLOPPED ONTO THE COUCH** in my office with a look of satisfaction on her face. In her hand, she clutched a brand-new iPhone.

For several months, I had been working with her parents to

---

8    Lenore Skenazy, "Why I Let My 9-Year-Old Ride the Subway Alone," *New York Sun*, April 1, 2008, https://www.nysun.com/article/opinion-why-i-let-my-9-year-old-ride-subway-alone.

support them in their desire to delay smartphone access. They were concerned that their daughter, already very anxious and sensitive, might have trouble with the responsibility and burden that came with such open access to the internet and social media. Maria, now a sixth grader, had long felt like she was the only one without a smartphone and disagreed with her parents' decision to delay.

We had been making good progress. Her parents were well informed about the risks of smartphone addiction and social media, but they, like so many parents, struggled with not wanting their daughter to feel left out. To unite their local community, Maria's mother, Ann, had even arranged for me to teach workshops to a group of parents from her school in hopes that they might support one another in delaying access. But something had shifted, and Ann now wanted to meet with me to talk about the change.

A few days prior to our meeting, Ann emailed me a video of an ecstatic Maria unwrapping her first iPhone. With a twinge of guilt noticeable in her message, Ann admitted that despite their efforts, they had caved, and would I be willing to talk this over with the family?

I agreed.

As Maria and her parents settled in, almost as if on cue, her brand-new smartphone burst to life. Suddenly, Maria's gleeful expression turned to one of horror as she glanced down at the ringing phone in her hand and gasped, "I don't know this number! I don't know anyone in this city! Who is calling me from there? How did they get my number?"

Maria's parents and I watched Maria's mood change instantaneously. Even though I had expected some adjustments for Maria in having her own phone, I was still surprised by the extremity of her reaction. Her parents and I tried to reassure Maria that it was likely a wrong number or spam and that it was okay to ignore calls from people she didn't know. We told her this kind of thing happens all the time with smartphones.

Maria calmed down a bit but was rattled.

The irony of this moment was not lost on me. We had gathered to talk about how to manage the responsibility of a smartphone while protecting Maria's mental health, yet a simple wrong number had sent her spiraling into near panic.

Breathing deeply, we regrouped and began to talk about the situation that had led Maria's parents to abandon the plan to delay the smartphone. Ann told me that a few weeks prior, Maria had gone skiing with three friends. At one point, Maria got separated from her friends and didn't know how to find them. In tears, she had returned to the lodge, and it was some time before they were reunited. That evening, Maria, still scared and upset about the experience, told her parents that if she had only had a phone at that moment, she would have been able to reach her friends and avoided feeling so scared and alone.

Maria's parents were convinced: this seemed to be a matter of safety. They decided to get her a smartphone.

Before we move on, I want to state up front that there is enough parent shaming in the world to last several lifetimes, so this is *not* an indictment of Maria's parents. They were doing the best they could with the information they had. And many parents find themselves in situations similar to that of Maria's parents. Though the details may change, experiences like getting lost on a ski slope have prompted numerous parents to see the smartphone as the next logical step in helping their children. Although their methods of protecting their kids can vary greatly, most parents want to keep their children safe from harm; this is completely understandable.

But are there drawbacks to always rescuing and protecting our children? And how on earth do we manage that when it comes to digital safety?

## CULTIVATING RESILIENCE

A generation ago, we talked about helicopter parents. These were the parents who would rush a forgotten lunch to school or help with a school project so their children wouldn't suffer the pain of a low grade. Today's version of a helicopter parent is the snowplow parent, who plows away obstacles *before* their children encounter them in hopes that these efforts will protect them from pain.

Though well intended, such behavior prevents children from practicing problem-solving and handling hardship—experiences that increase their resilience and fortitude and constitute the 21st-century skills that actually matter for future success. A healthy childhood *needs* to include some challenges and obstacles. A wise mental health practitioner I know once told me, "Childhood is fraught with pain and suffering. And healthy adults are not the ones who went through childhood unscathed; they are the ones who were scathed a little bit" and got through it.

Snowplow parents truly want to shield their children from suffering. But this overprotective behavior is a narrow and problematic way of thinking. The snowplow parent is thinking of their *own* anxieties about childhood without seeing the lifetime that unfolded in the years following. What snowplow parents lose sight of is that most of the obstacles and challenges of childhood are what taught them important coping skills and built their resilience. However, we aren't always willing or able to unpack our childhoods even though they hold many valuable lessons for us as parents.

But if we step back for a moment and look not at what we perceive is gained by our snowplow parenting efforts (i.e., supposed protection) but rather at what is lost, we might come to a different conclusion about what's best for our children. When we plow away the obstacles that lie before our children, we rob them of the opportunity to try something difficult on their own and the glorious feeling of triumph when successful. We give them the false impression that loss and hardship are something they shouldn't have to confront, when suffering and challenge are actually part of the human experience, no matter how great we are as parents. By not allowing them to struggle through difficult moments, we teach them that we do not trust their abilities, which in turn leads them to question themselves: "My parents don't think I can handle this. Maybe I can't." We also model that rescuing people from hard moments is always good rather than helping them experience the value of learning through discomfort.

Ultimately, when we are snowplow parents, we can unintentionally create harm for our children. Our kids will not learn—or will be unable to learn—how to solve problems or deal with challenges, something we absolutely hope for them as future adults. So let's consider something for a moment: What if, instead of giving Maria a smartphone, her parents had waited, helping her see that her experience on the slopes was an opportunity to learn and grow? What if enduring those moments of fear helped their child increase her resilience for the future? That trade-off between Maria encountering moments of uncertainty plus her parents feeling guilty about her fear and Maria building long-term self-reliance suggests that giving the smartphone was perhaps not the best next step.

## FEARING WORST-CASE SCENARIOS IN THE DIGITAL AGE

Richard Branson, perhaps best known as the founder of the Virgin Group, is a successful entrepreneur whose estimated worth today is in the billions of dollars. But as a child, he was painfully shy. He didn't like to talk to strangers and would hide in his mother's skirts. However, his mother was concerned that his shyness would be debilitating to him as he got older, and she didn't want that for him—she wasn't a snowplow parent.

When he was just six years old, in a rather unconventional parenting decision, Branson's mother decided to drop him off three miles from home and make him find his own way back. She told him he would have to talk to strangers to get directions to get home.

I know many of you reading these words might be hyperventilating a bit. Drop a six-year-old off? Alone? Three miles from home?! That's neglect! That's abandonment! That's traumatic! Perhaps. Times were different back then. This was England in 1956, after all, and research on trauma and childhood was not yet at the forefront of people's minds. Parenting styles were very different. It's also true that today's parents have sometimes been reported for letting their children play alone on a playground or walk home alone from school when that used to be very much the norm.

But these shifts aside, here's the important part of the story: it worked. Branson discovered that he could do something really, really difficult. In fact, it took him hours to get home, and his mother was "apoplectic" (his words) when he finally did arrive, but neither had considered that he would discover many wonderful things along his journey. The experience ultimately changed *both* of them. Branson's mother believed in his ability to get home, and her belief in his ability gave him the confidence he needed to do it—even if the journey was scary. Even better, the future entrepreneur discovered that "growth happens when you put yourself outside your comfort zone." Branson credits this experience with helping him better interact with others and more clearly express himself. Isn't that what we want for our children?

If you were to google "children walking home alone traumatic stories" right now, you might find several horrific examples. You wouldn't be wrong that sometimes bad things do happen. However, if your instinctive response to reading Branson's story is to immediately find the extreme exceptions that ended in catastrophe, you are already proving the point: screens won't make children safer.

As adults, and even more so as parents, we are susceptible to the bad, the scary, the horrifying stories. And more than in any previous generation, we have instant, 24/7 access to hundreds of thousands of stories because they make for effective clickbait. But when we were growing up, consuming news was entirely different. A morning or evening newspaper might arrive on our doorsteps. Only a few television networks existed, and perhaps we watched the five o'clock evening news. Maybe we listened to the radio for local updates. Breaking news events were consigned to these time-bound experiences with rare exceptions. If something traumatic happened, we didn't learn about it at 11:00 p.m. because we were scrolling through Twitter; we went to bed and read about it the next morning in the newspaper or heard about it on the radio. Any spike in news-related anxiety was limited to the availability of updates, which were specific, scheduled, and predictable.

The challenge today is that our 24/7 news cycle means we remain in a state of hyperarousal, finely attuned to the breaking news headlines that might range from political mayhem to celebrity news updates. Both are given equal, hyperbolic attention, even if they don't affect our lives or our world in the same way. Consequently, with our own heightened parental attunement to this constant barrage of information, we consume the opinions of others in the form of social media posts or news commentary. We spend less time reading in-depth journalism and more time scrolling bite-sized summaries. We engage with accounts that are in line with the beliefs we hold and share content that justifies our fears.

As we doomscroll before bed, our anxiety levels rise, and we begin to assume the worst lies ahead for ourselves and for our children. We read about kids in frightening situations, begin to believe that smartphones will help keep our children safe, and rush out to buy them an iPhone at the next opportunity—only to open them up to the same cycle of clickbait headlines that increased our own anxiety in the first place.

A lot of factors, including both exaggerated headlines and legitimately disturbing events, contribute to our parental fears. Most recently, a global pandemic turned our world upside down. But in the coming years, new crises will emerge. As we look to this inevitable future, does giving our children access to smart devices make them safer? Or are we making our children *less* safe by denying them the ability to build resilience through normal life experiences?

To unpack this, we need to look at two distinct words: "scary" and "dangerous."

## SCARY VERSUS DANGEROUS

As a former English teacher, I believe words and language matter a great deal to our understanding of the world, and I am a big fan of unpacking the roots and meanings of words. For example, let's look at *scary* and *dangerous*. *Scary* is an adjective that means "causing fright." An earlier form of this word, *sker*, is the Middle English word for "fear" or "dread." *Dangerous* means "able or likely to inflict injury, harm, pain, or loss." The origin of this word is the Old French word *dangeros*, meaning "power to harm."

Scary things often make the headlines. We read and hear a lot about events that are scary even though the likelihood of their happening is low. And because of our constant exposure to these scary but ultimately rare experiences (these types of headlines are the most successful clickbait, after all), our perception is skewed: we end up thinking the scary things are actually dangerous.

But they are not. Something that is dangerous—but common— rarely makes the headlines. Dangerous situations or incidents are actually detrimental to our health and well-being, but because common things, even if they're likely harmful, are not very clickbaity and therefore don't appear in our newsfeeds, our perception of these dangers minimizes their seriousness. We don't worry about dangerous things the way we worry about scary things.

Here are a few examples:

| SCARY | DANGEROUS |
|---|---|
| Shark attacks | Drowning in bathtubs |
| Airplane crashes | Car crashes |
| Getting lost on a ski slope | Relying on a smartphone to problem-solve |
| Not being able to contact a parent when anxious | Not knowing other ways to ask for help |
| Feeling like the only kid without social media | Having social media that damages mental health and worsens the fear of missing out |
| School shootings | Gun violence |
| Having moments of normal childhood struggle | Never learning to persevere through normal moments of struggle |
| Having anxiety about the world | Being inundated with news headlines on a smartphone that further increases anxiety |
| Kidnapping | Predatory grooming in online games and chats |
| Getting lost on the way home from school | Getting lost in the comment threads on social media accounts |

This is where the decision to give our kids smartphones requires a necessary shift in our thinking: smartphones (and smartwatches) are not scary; they are dangerous. And when 20% of eight-year-olds and more than half of 11-year-olds have smartphones, we need to consider the very real harm such device use poses to our children.

For example, Roblox is currently the most popular game in the United States for children 5–12 years old, with 52 million daily active users, but predators are known to hang out in games that children frequent. Meanwhile, social media companies know their products are harmful to young people: Meta's own internal research, leaked by whistleblower Frances Haugen to the *Wall Street Journal*, shows that they have known since 2018 that Instagram harms teen girls, and the U.S. military prohibits service members from using TikTok on government-issued devices because the platform is owned by ByteDance, a Chinese AI company.[9] Technology companies mine personal information on children to intentionally push "personalized" content, increasing the likelihood they will stay on the device longer. Even EdTech platforms, used by millions during remote learning, collect data about children, often without parental consent or even knowledge.

Beyond the dangers of predators, reduced self-esteem, and privacy leaks, smartphones and excessive screentime have been shown to impact our children's health in other ways in the past several years. For instance, research by Victoria L. Dunckley, a developmental child psychiatrist and author of *Reset Your Child's Brain*, has highlighted increased rates of psychiatric diagnoses (e.g., ADHD, depression, anxiety, tics, and autism), chronic medical conditions (e.g., obesity and high cholesterol), disability filings (mostly for neuropsychological issues), and medication use (e.g., stimulants

---

9    Georgia Wells, Jeff Horwitz, and Deepa Seetharaman, "Facebook Knows Instagram Is Toxic for Teen Girls," *Wall Street Journal*, September 14, 2021, https://www.wsj.com/articles/facebook-knows-instagram-is-toxic-for-teen-girls-company-documents-show-11631620739.

for ADHD and antipsychotics) among children. She has also noted increases in adverse effects on their mental health, sleep, weight, and creative play.[10]

And it's not just the experts who are concerned about this; parental anecdotes are equally revealing. Many parents tell me, "I wish I had waited on giving them a smartphone. I wish I hadn't given them social media access yet. I wish I had known then what I know now." When our children are young, we don't always know what is coming. And because things have changed so rapidly, it is even more difficult to know what's right or good about screentime and parenting and what to avoid or limit.

## SMARTWATCHES, "CHILD-FRIENDLY" PHONES, AND SAFETY

The story of Maria and her family's decision to get her a smartphone is representative of the experiences of so many parents with tweens. But there is also a growing trend among families with younger children who see the smartwatch as a safe precursor to the smartphone.

Simplified versions of smartphones are now available from companies such as Bark, Pinwheel, Troomi, and Gabb. These "child-friendly" smartphones purport to offer a safer phone experience by offering streamlined platforms, providing content filters, limiting apps or social media, or allowing parents to track their children's location—though their capabilities vary wildly depending on the device and plan.

Like other forms of parental controls, however, there are some limitations to these alternative devices. I've heard from many parents whose children see these "safe" smartphones as childish or embarrassing.

---

10    Victoria L. Dunckley, *Reset Your Child's Brain* (Novato, CA: New World Library, July 2015).

Sometimes children pretend to use these devices to comply with their parents' rules but then buy burner phones or use friends' smartphones without their parents' knowledge. Some of the apps available allow children to hide social media accounts in fake apps disguised to look like calculators. Other apps show parents a false geolocation, disguising their child's actual location. And most of these devices cannot monitor in-app content thanks to, for example, the refusal of social media companies to allow for this. Finally, providing children with a kid version of a device that is designed to look like a smartphone can appear to be about "fitting in"—which should never be a reason to give such a technologically advanced tool to a child.

For some families, a smartwatch or smartphone alternative might be useful. However, it is not a route I currently recommend or have used personally, in part because I believe the focus must first and foremost be on the relationships we have with our children, and in part because young children simply don't need devices.

In general, while child-friendly phones and smartwatches may be better than an unregulated smartphone in the hands of an elementary school student, one important factor that doesn't often get discussed is that all these devices are highly distracting. When my 11-year-old (who does not have her own smartphone) wanted to text friends, I allowed her to use my phone. She was added to a group chat, which I allowed, and which she knew I could see and read. What shocked both of us, however, was how distracting the influx of texts was. In one 30-minute span, she received 243 texts. All the other issues of smart devices aside, this alone is reason enough to delay access. Who can focus with that level of constant interruption? As a fully grown adult, even I was completely distracted. Thankfully, she felt this way too and has since declined to participate in large group chats.

As parents grapple with the question of when to give their child a device, especially when they are younger, the smartwatch or smartphone alternative is a seemingly viable option. But the concern isn't so much whether a smartphone is better than a smartwatch or alternative device for a young child; the focus should be on the reason a parent feels compelled to give a device in the first place.

I regularly ask this question of parents. The top two responses I hear are "I want to be able to reach my child/have my child reach me" and "I want to keep them safe." These responses are understandable: from a parent's perspective, giving a child a smart device does make it easier to reach our child. But smartphones and smartwatches do not make our children safer because these devices are actually dangerous. Too much access too soon to smartphones, smartwatches, the internet, online gaming, and social media increases our child's risk of experiencing actual harm in the form of exposure to pornography, violence, addictive algorithms, cyberbullying, harmful content, dis- and misinformation, and sexual predators. Not only does a smartphone or smartwatch not keep our child safer; it decreases their ability to focus and be present while exposing them to legitimately dangerous content and people on the internet.

The inherent dangers of the rising use of smartphones and smartwatches among children at younger and younger ages become even more evident in the changing communications coming from our schools, which are having to adjust their own rules about these products. Just a short time ago, elementary schools didn't even have policies about students' personal devices; now, forms for field trips and school outings ask children to leave smartphones and smartwatches at home. My daughter's principal sent an email to remind parents to have their children keep devices turned off and stored in backpacks for the duration of the school day because too many were going off during class and interrupting lessons. This was a K–5 school.

So is a smartwatch really all that different from a smartphone? Besides the obvious physical differences (wearing it on our body instead of carrying it in our pocket), the smartwatch might also be easier to monitor and moderate from a parent's perspective. But a smartwatch is really just a small smartphone on our wrist, even if we want to convince ourselves that it isn't. And that means these supposedly alternative devices still present many of the same dangers as a smartphone. Their perceived benefit—making our children safer—is about alleviating *our* fears and anxieties about our children's experience of the real world, not theirs. But they still make our kids prone to distraction, even when locked down or monitored. They still rob children of the opportunity to problem-solve and build resilience, including on school trips, where our kids get to practice being away from home, in preparation for young adulthood. And smartwatches give parents only the illusion of safety while blinding us to very real dangers, from privacy and data violations and exposure to eating disorder content to cyberbullying, predatory groomers, and sextortion.

## "BUT MY KID IS DIFFERENT"

A lot of parents want to believe that their situation is unique. *Their* child has a specific reason to need a smartwatch at a certain age. These parents say they have "done the research" and feel like this is the best fit for their family. These parents might even be judgmental of other parents' decisions about screen use or smartphone access. When we want to feel justified in our decisions, we look for ways to differentiate ourselves.

However, with very few exceptions (e.g., using a smartphone as a medical device for a diabetic child), these justifications aren't warranted. Our children are not safer because they have smart devices. In fact, we do them a disservice by thinking that they are. Both anecdotes and research definitively show that our children are harmed by excessive screen use and early access to smart devices. So what are some of the best practices that we can put in place to actually change things?

## WE NEED PARENTING, NOT PARENTAL CONTROLS

Parents who come to me for help hope that parental controls—the apps, software, monitoring or filtering services, special routers, or limits set by a parent's phone—are the answer to all their problems. Parents think that with the right filters and features, their children will be able to put down their devices, enjoy family time, and keep relationships strong and healthy. Some even see parental controls as a release from mentoring and teaching. It's probably why I am asked this question all the time: "What parental controls do you recommend?"

The reality is that I don't recommend parental controls. Instead, I recommend parenting.

I'm being cheeky. The tech industry would love for parents to feel responsible for all family screentime conflicts so they don't have to be accountable, but technology companies absolutely should be. Experts such as author Nir Eyal blame parental failures for why children are addicted to devices. News media perpetuates this message as well, and often nonparents, even well-meaning ones, say, "Just tell your kids no. How hard is that?" But as parents can attest, it's virtually impossible.

Parental controls can be one tool in our toolbox. If they work for your family, that's fine—keep them. However, simply using parental controls does not exempt us from teaching our children about how to be safe online, how to deal with scary situations or images, or how to balance tech use intentionally. Parental controls are imperfect at best, and, ironically, they can even make parenting in the digital age harder.

Our job is to be the parent. As Devorah Heitner, author of *Growing Up in Public: Coming of Age in a Digital World*, says, we must be the mentors, not just the monitors.[11] After talking to many parents and

---

11   Devorah Heitner, *Growing Up in Public* (New York, NY: TarcherPerigee, September 2023).

hearing so many stories about parental control workarounds and misfires, I've come up with a list of 10 reasons that parental controls aren't the be-all and end-all we wish them to be:

1. **Children find workarounds.** Always. Social media parenting groups are full of examples of parents who thought they had things locked down only to discover their kids adjusted the clock to increase screentime limits, used Google Docs as a chatting platform, or found a backdoor to TikTok through Pinterest. (Remember how we used to program the VCR for our parents? No matter the generation, kids tend to be savvier than adults when it comes to adapting to new technology.)

2. **Children are not small adults.** Children cannot monitor their own use or understand that what they post online is permanent and public. Our child might be brilliant, but their brain will still not be fully developed until they are in their 20s or even 30s. That means teens can't be expected to self-regulate yet either. Parental controls do not teach children how to self-regulate.

3. **Parental controls are a ton of work for parents.** There is a lot of setup and maintenance. These apps are cumbersome, complicated, confusing, and designed to put the burden of monitoring onto parents. One parent told me it felt like a second full-time job just to manage the parental controls. Additionally, when parents rely heavily on parental controls, parents spend more time looking at their own phones just to monitor their children's screentime.

4. **It's weird to use technology to solve a problem created by technology.** Tech companies make money off the time we spend engaging with digital content. They also make money off the apps we download and the devices we buy to monitor and

manage our children's use of technology. We should be pushing back on Big Tech for creating products that refuse to keep children's development and best interests at heart in the first place.

5. **Parental controls reinforce inequities.** Higher-quality parental controls cost money, expertise, time, and tech-savvy. Expensive routers and filtering software require subscriptions. Some families simply cannot afford or manage these protections. The children of families with the resources to add (even a weak layer of) protection benefit, while those who lack access are exposed to more harm.

6. **Don't be fooled. Tech companies are not being altruistic.** Just watch the many congressional hearings in which senators and representatives interviewed executives of YouTube, Instagram, and other tech giants: all of them deflected responsibility for protecting children onto the parents. Tech companies tell us they're making changes to help parents and better protect children, but it's not because they care; they are legally obligated to do so. The Children's Online Privacy Protection Act of 1998 requires that tech companies make some effort to protect underage users, but corporations are doing the bare minimum. Moreover, if parental controls actually worked effectively, tech companies would be less profitable, so it is unlikely they will willingly make changes anytime soon.

7. **Tech companies want parents to feel guilty.** It is much easier to put the burden of managing screentime and protecting children on parents than to change a profitable business model. Parents already have plenty to feel guilty about. By telling parents, "This is your fault," tech companies deflect responsibility and can maintain the narrative that this is about faulty parenting, not intentional design.

8. **Parental controls do not monitor in-app content.** I want to shout this from the rooftops. Parents download or purchase parental controls thinking that in-app content will be monitored or filtered. IT. IS. NOT. Tech companies make it so that third parties cannot monitor in-app content; if they could, the algorithms would decrease the amount of time children spend engaging with their product. A monitoring tool might alert a parent if *an app* is downloaded, but rarely will it allow parents to monitor *the content within the app* once it is downloaded.

9. **Children learn the wrong lesson from parental controls.** Different parents worry about different online dangers, whether it's exposure to pornography, violence, content that promotes eating disorders, self-harm, or suicide. But no app, control, software, or router is a replacement for teaching children what to do when they see something that is scary or worrisome. We don't build relationships with our children to keep them from experiencing or seeing harmful content; we build relationships with our children so that *when* that happens, they come to us for help. Unfortunately, when we rely solely on parental controls without teaching children about trust and consent, children may feel more inclined to seek answers on the internet instead of from a trusted adult.

10. **Parental controls cannot replace real-life relationships.** Parental controls are not tools that teach our children about safe searching, privacy protection, or media literacy. Teaching these topics is the job of parents (and schools, especially as they use more tech). Parenting is not something we can outsource to an app. In fact, parental controls lull us into a false sense of security: "If we just have *X*, our child will be safe." If we want our children to think critically, ask for help when they need it, and know what

to do when—not if—they see pornographic or violent content, we must focus on building our relationships first.

Well-intentioned parents think they are doing everything right until suddenly they aren't. Parental controls can be one layer of protection, but don't have high expectations of them. They are not the panacea we want them to be. Until the tech business model changes, the onus will continue to be on parents to fix, prevent, and solve these problems.

## DISCERNING THE SCARY FROM THE DANGEROUS

Parenting in the digital age feels scary. Our use of screens and access to social media tap into our fears about the world and justify our worries, after all. But without applying wisdom or critical thinking—important tools in parenting—we make decisions about our children's screen use based on things that feel scary but are not truly dangerous. For example, we give kids phones because we are scared about dangerous things happening to them in the real world, such as getting lost on a ski slope, when, in fact, giving them early access to the digital world is a real cause of harm.

When it comes to giving our kids devices, we must override our own brains' propensity to seek out the scary without acknowledging the truly dangerous. For example, we have to remind ourselves that children today are much safer in the real world than any previous generation, despite those frightening headlines. This kind of mindset shift is challenging; after all, it is normal and natural to be afraid of scary things. It may also be unpopular—to our children or to our parenting peers. But making choices about screen access that are different from what other families do doesn't negate that reality. Our reaction to scary things cannot be to give our children smart devices or social media access before they are developmentally ready. That choice solves an unlikely risk that can expose them to real danger.

## DAMNED IF WE DO, DAMNED IF WE DON'T

No matter what, whether and when we give our kid a smartphone or access to social media, they will be affected by our decision. This is part of what makes parenting in the digital age so challenging: we feel damned if we do and damned if we don't. Even children without smartphones or social media are peripherally affected by the social climate. Other children talk about their tech-based experiences at school, and our children will come home with questions. They will see or share friends' devices. They will encounter sketchy content on YouTube at school. These are normal childhood experiences today, whether we've allowed smartphones or smartwatches or not.

Families are going to make different choices about when to give devices. And knowing how to respond firmly when our children ask us, "When do we get phones?" is difficult. Even in my household, despite our family rule about delaying until eighth grade, my fifth grader has started a full-court press for a device of her own. It may be a long few years. We will have to hold out while trying to navigate social dynamics and communication needs. And I am not fooled into thinking it will be easy or make us popular parents. But we can be intentional in how we go about it.

## A DIFFERENT APPROACH

Without judgment (because we know how judgmental parents can be of other parents), let's go back to Maria's story. Maria's parents felt that they were addressing their daughter's anxiety by giving her a smartphone. Their fear about her getting lost on the ski slope ultimately trumped their concerns about giving her a smartphone. But let's reflect on the situation: Maria came home from the ski slope, distraught and scared. She'd had a frightening experience and felt overwhelmed about how to handle it. Already an anxious child, this only magnified her fears.

Although her parents had spent a lot of time researching and learning about smartphone risks and safety, one thing that might have gotten overlooked in their efforts was to teach Maria how to problem-solve *in the real world* first. What if, before going skiing, Maria's parents had role-played with her and asked, "What should you do if you get separated from your friends on the ski slope?" Together, they could have brainstormed ideas: she could look for a member of the ski patrol and ask them for help. She could approach a parent skiing with their child and ask to use their phone. Or she could've used a landline at the lodge to call her parents.

There are a few skills embedded in these options that require some preteaching: Does Maria know how to identify ski patrol? Does she know her friends' phone numbers by heart? Does she know how to use a landline? Does she know her parents' phone numbers?

It's absurd to think that we can plan for every potential moment of adversity; that simply isn't possible. But part of the work of parenting is preparing our children for real-world experiences: how to order food in a restaurant, how to behave in a movie theater, how to say thank you, how to be a good team player, how to ask for help when they need it. Whether we are aware of it or not, we are constantly teaching our children life skills.

One way to approach the decision of whether to provide a child with a smart device might be to notice the fears about *not* providing it. What would be scary about not having a device? What would be a parallel example of something truly dangerous?

## THE PROBLEM-SOLVING SKILLS KIDS NEED

If you want to give your child a smart device because you are worried about your child getting lost on the way home from school, for example, make a list of the actions you might take to help them prepare for that possibility:

- Walk the route with them several times.
- Point out landmarks, friendly neighbors, or businesses.
- Have them memorize your phone number and put it on a piece of paper in their backpack.
- Talk about what to do if someone makes them feel uncomfortable or afraid.
- Teach them about traffic safety and where to cross streets.
- Show them why it is important to have their head up and eyes alert when near moving traffic.
- Let your child know you trust them to do this big step and that you believe in their ability to do it.

If action is the antidote to anxiety, write yourself a prescription and get to work! Modeling for our children how to handle moments of struggle also shows them that when we're prepared (as much as we can be), we can face and survive scary situations.

Being afraid is not always a bad thing. We can learn a lot from our fear. But letting our own anxieties about our children get in the way of intentional decision-making, which translates into their lack of self-confidence or resilience, can be dangerous—if not deadly.

## TL;DR

- Less is more. Later is better. Prioritize relationships over screens.

- Smartphones and smartwatches do not make a child safer.

- Snowplow parenting prevents children from building critical skills that make them safer.

- Parental controls are not the solution; being intentional about our use of technology is.

CHAPTER 3

# ALIGNING SCREEN USE WITH FAMILY VALUES

The question isn't so much, "Are you parenting the
right way?" as it is, "Are you the adult that you
want your child to grow up to be?"

—BRENÉ BROWN, AUTHOR OF *DARING GREATLY*[12]

## REPLACE JUDGMENT WITH CURIOSITY

Many years ago, I took a mindfulness class with my husband. (This, of course, was before we had children, when we had time to take a mindfulness class.) Something the teacher said that day stayed with me, and it now serves as a core element in my tech-intentional approach to screentime: she invited us to replace judgment with curiosity—for ourselves, for our children, and for others.

I loved this idea so much that I decided to have it engraved on a key chain for my husband. When I picked up the finished gift, I

---

12  Brené Brown, *Daring Greatly* (New York, NY: Avery, April 2015).

showed it to my cousin, who was visiting. She took it in her hands, read it, looked up with an amused expression on her face, and said, "Emily, you spelled 'judgment' *and* 'curiosity' wrong."

My jaw dropped. Not only had I filled out the paperwork myself (so I couldn't blame the faulty spelling on the engraver), but I was also an English teacher at the time. What an absolute embarrassment! Perfectionism was my historical go-to, but this was hardly the perfect gift. I was mortified.

Yet what an opportunity to practice this very sentiment. In this awkward moment, I could replace judgment (or *judgement*, which I later learned has two acceptable spellings—no judg[e]ment to my cousin, who was only trying to help!) of myself with curiosity (okay, to be fair, *curiousity* is not a variant spelling). I could admit that even as an English teacher, I made mistakes. I could model for my students that adults are imperfect humans. I could show myself that a spelling error wasn't cause for an emotional breakdown. After all, we learn when we *make* mistakes, not when we avoid them.

Eventually, I gave the key chain to my husband, typos and all. I felt it was symbolic to acknowledge, to myself as much as to him, that I wasn't perfect and that was okay.

And at the end of the day, it was actually pretty funny.

## THE COMPETITIVE SPORT OF PARENTING

When it comes to parenting in the digital age, screentime is a topic that is fraught with judgment—for ourselves, for other parents, and for other children.

Before the pandemic, many parents worked hard to set time limits and restrictions on children's personal devices. But following the exponential rise of remote learning and the isolation of the pandemic, children's use of screentime increased, and the battles became harder:

"Everyone else has a phone now!" "How else will I connect with my friends?" "I have to use the computer for my schoolwork!" "You're on your laptop for work all day!"

Many pandemic parents, stressed and overwhelmed, just gave in—or gave up. It didn't seem like a fight we could win. Plus, so much of schoolwork required digital technology, and it *did* seem like everyone else had a smartphone or social media accounts. And as parents, if we could work from home, we were guilty of using our own devices all day for work while trying to stay on top of everything else.

I have so much empathy for those who have parented through a pandemic. None of us had that on our parenting bingo card. We had to do something really, really hard that we were not prepared for. It was scary. We did our best. And despite that, a lot of screentime rules did slide. A lot of fights just did not seem worth having. Instead, we triaged.

But in the aftermath of this phase of the pandemic, we were left to reenter a new normal—to establish new limits for children who were three years wiser and in new stages of development than when they entered the pandemic. We had to accept that the millions of dollars that schools invested in digital technology for remote learning meant that schools were going to keep using digital technology.

We had to decide whether maybe, after all, there *were* some fights still worth having. But which ones, and how could we tell?

## IDENTIFYING FAMILY VALUES

Before we change a single thing about screentime in our homes, we need to start by identifying our family's top values. Why? Because once we have clarity about those values, we can fold in our screentime rules and limits. That is, we can make these choices because they are in alignment with what we feel is important in our family.

Becoming a tech-intentional parent and finding balance with screentime always comes back to values. Even in dual-household families, identifying values is important to establishing screentime balance. It's okay if the values are different in different households. The important thing is that we communicate those values clearly to the children and adults who are involved in following and honoring them.

Sometimes, this may not be possible. Some parents differ so widely in their beliefs that we can't reconcile them or find common ground. For example, one parent will say, "Well, it's not *me* who has the problem enforcing screentime limits; it's my spouse!" or "I have rules in *my* house, but when she goes to her dad's, all bets are off." That can be challenging—and not just for screentime issues. But when parenting around screentime feels hard, it is important to remember that we can only control what happens in our own households.

## Defining Values

Values are individual beliefs that motivate us to act in a certain way. They serve as guides for how we behave and what we think is important.

Values can be rooted in religious faith, but they do not have to be. Spirituality, in addition to things like culture and politics, can shape our values. The approach offered in this book is secular, but it can certainly blend into a family's religious belief system. Take from it what resonates and add it to the systems you already have in place.

Our personal values are also rooted in our family of origin's belief systems. How we were raised and what we were taught by adults when we were children influence the beliefs we hold today. Sometimes, when our beliefs or values differ from our family of origin, we can experience tension or conflict.

When it comes to screentime, there are many instances of clashing values. For example, grandparents might think parents are giving children way too much access to devices, or they may be guilty of providing excess screentime against their adult children's wishes. One parent might think concerns about tech use are overwrought, while a spouse or coparent might be gravely concerned. And children themselves have a lot of opinions and beliefs about tech use and its importance and value to their lives. In other words, when it comes to values and screentime, it's complicated.

This chapter will help you identify the values that are most important to the families you lead. Being tech-intentional focuses on values as the anchor of our approach to screentime. Recall the definition: "Being tech-intentional means using screen-based technologies . . . in ways that align with our *values*." To become tech-intentional in the way we parent, we must have clearly defined values to build on.

## Exercise: Identify Your Values

This exercise can be done by yourself, with your coparent or caregiver, and even with your children, depending on their ages. The following is a list of values; you can start with this, or feel free to create a list of your own. Read through it, and circle the values that jump out to you. Then, go back through and highlight the ones that feel most important to you personally. There are no right answers here; try to stay neutral and nonjudgmental.

| | | | | |
|---|---|---|---|---|
| Acceptance | Alertness | Awareness | Brilliance | Certainty |
| Accomplishment | Altruism | Balance | Calm | Challenge |
| Accountability | Ambition | Beauty | Candor | Charity |
| Accuracy | Amusement | Being the best | Capability | Clarity |
| Achievement | Assertiveness | Belonging | Career | Cleanliness |
| Adaptability | Attentiveness | Boldness | Carefulness | Cleverness |
| Adventure | Authenticity | Bravery | Caring | Collaboration |

*continued*

| | | | | |
|---|---|---|---|---|
| Comfort | Exploration | Intelligence | Prosperity | Talent |
| Commitment | Expressiveness | Intensity | Purpose | Teamwork |
| Common sense | Fairness | Intuition | Quality | Temperance |
| Communication | Faith | Irreverence | Realism | Thoroughness |
| Community | Family | Job security | Reason | Thoughtfulness |
| Compassion | Fame | Joy | Recognition | Thrift |
| Competence | Fearlessness | Justice | Recreation | Time |
| Concentration | Feelings | Kindness | Reliability | Timeliness |
| Confidence | Ferocity | Knowledge | Resilience | Tolerance |
| Connection | Fidelity | Lawfulness | Resourcefulness | Toughness |
| Consciousness | Focus | Leadership | Respect | Tradition |
| Consistency | Foresight | Learning | Responsibility | Tranquility |
| Contentment | Fortitude | Legacy | Restraint | Transparency |
| Contribution | Freedom | Leisure | Results | Travel |
| Control | Friendship | Liberty | Reverence | Trust |
| Conviction | Fun | Logic | Rigor | Truth |
| Cooperation | Future generations | Love | Risk-taking | Understanding |
| Courage | Generosity | Loyalty | Safety | Uniqueness |
| Courtesy | Genius | Making a difference | Satisfaction | Unity |
| Creation | Giving | Mastery | Security | Usefulness |
| Creativity | Goodness | Maturity | Self-discipline | Valor |
| Credibility | Grace | Meaning | Self-expression | Victory |
| Curiosity | Gratitude | Moderation | Self-reliance | Vigor |
| Decisiveness | Greatness | Motivation | Self-respect | Vision |
| Dedication | Grit | Nature | Sensitivity | Vitality |
| Dependability | Growth | Openness | Serenity | Vulnerability |
| Determination | Happiness | Optimism | Service | Wealth |
| Development | Hard work | Order | Sharing | Welcoming |
| Devotion | Harmony | Organization | Silence | Well-being |
| Dignity | Health | Originality | Simplicity | Wholeheartedness |
| Discipline | Home | Parenting | Sincerity | Winning |
| Discovery | Honesty | Passion | Skill | Wisdom |
| Diversity | Honor | Patience | Solitude | Wonder |
| Drive | Hope | Peace | Spirit | |
| Efficiency | Humility | Performance | Spirituality | |
| Empathy | Imagination | Perseverance | Spontaneity | |
| Empowerment | Improvement | Persistence | Sportsmanship | |
| Endurance | Inclusion | Personal fulfillment | Stability | |
| Energy | Independence | Playfulness | Status | |
| Enjoyment | Individuality | Poise | Stewardship | |
| Enthusiasm | Initiative | Potential | Strength | |
| Environment | Innovation | Power | Structure | |
| Equality | Inquisitiveness | Presence | Success | |
| Ethics | Insightfulness | Pride | Support | |
| Excellence | Inspiration | Productivity | Surprise | |
| Experience | Integrity | Professionalism | Sustainability | |

If you haven't already narrowed your choices down to three or fewer, try that now. Picking a small number doesn't mean you don't have more than three values, but it *will* make it easier for you to ground your screentime rules in the ones that are most important.

Have your family members do the same. It's okay if you and your loved ones have different answers. The goal is to find some common ground and think about which value is the most important to your household.

As a family, share why you picked the values you did. See whether there are common themes. Again, different family members may highlight different values. Are there similarities? Which ones overlap? Are you surprised by the variability or similarity? Remember to replace judgment with curiosity.

## Helping Children Understand Values

It can be difficult for children to understand what we mean when we say "values." Start with the previous definitions. If you need additional prompts to help your children understand what you mean, here are some prompts; select the ones that feel most appropriate to their developmental skills:[13]

### Prompts for littles

- In our family, what is something that is not okay to do or say?

- What do you think we care about most in our home?

- What activities do we enjoy doing together?

- If we had free time, what would our family choose to do?

---

13  *Littles* refers to children roughly at a developmental stage of younger than 10 years old, and *middles* refers to those whose developmental stage is 10 years or older.

- If a friend came over and looked around our house, what might they think our family's interests are?

## Prompts for middles

- When we are being the best version of ourselves, how would you describe us?

- What do you think are the most important things to us as a family?

- When we have free time, what activities does our family like to do?

- If an alien from another planet landed in our living room and looked around, what do you think it would learn about us as a family?

- If your friends were to describe our family to their parents, what words do you think they would use?

Having this discussion with older children is highly valuable. Their insights are often far more aligned with ours than we might give them credit for. They also like being included in the decision-making and are more likely to have buy-in down the road when you do make screentime changes because the changes will make sense to them and they were a part of the process.

## Case Study: The Smith Family

When the Smith family first contacted me, they were having difficulty reestablishing screentime limits following the initial pandemic lockdown. Their tweens were on screens nonstop. One of the first exercises we did was to define their family's values. Sometimes this exercise can be done with all family members, and sometimes it works best if you start with just the parents. That's what Susan and Mike Smith decided to do.

Together, they went through the values list. For both, kindness rose to the top as the most important. Interestingly, both also acknowledged that just behind kindness was respect—and that as parents, they felt like they weren't modeling it in their interactions with their children because the conflicts around screen use had grown so tense.

We talked about what kindness might look like when it came to screentime, and Susan and Mike felt that how they currently talked with their kids about it probably didn't reflect this value. They realized that to make changes to the screentime rules, they were going to have to start by changing how they interacted with their children.

One strategy that we came up with was to be Switzerland. Because the interactions about screens were so fraught, the new goal for Susan and Mike was to try to remain as neutral as possible. This meant holding back the judgment, negativity, and anger when they were engaging with their children.

The second part of the strategy was to replace judgment with curiosity. This meant Susan and Mike would neutrally acknowledge their children's interests, ask open-ended questions, and acknowledge their children's feelings without judgment. This can be very challenging, especially when our own opinions and frustrations get wrapped up in the interactions we have with our children. It takes a lot of courage and effort to focus on our children's experiences and not our own reactions to those experiences. The hope was that by connecting first with their children, Susan and Mike could eventually move into a conversation about shifting screentime access.

For the Smith family, redefining their values meant choosing a guidepost for future conversations about screen use. Ultimately, acknowledging their values of kindness and respect meant reframing how they communicated with their children. Looking ahead, as their tweens turn into teens, focusing on their connection to their children in the context of kindness and respect will ultimately be more impactful for them than what specific time limits they set on screen use.

After our sessions concluded, Susan sent me an email. She wrote that our work together had allowed their family to "break this elephant-sized problem into manageable tasks" and "gave [us] a road map to follow as [we] encounter challenges down the road."

## BE THE PARENT

Several years ago, my husband, Ben, went into our son's room to help him fall asleep. Ben lay down on his back on the bed next to Max, but in his left hand, just below the edge of the bed, he was scrolling on his iPhone.

Max was quiet for a while, then sat up, turned to Ben, and said, "Daddy, I can't compete with your iPhone." It was a humbling parenting moment, but Max was right: kids can't, and shouldn't have to, compete with our devices for attention and connection. After that interaction, as a family, we decided that parents' devices were no longer allowed in the bedrooms.

Children hate hypocrisy. This doesn't mean we should never use our devices around them. But it should go without saying that if we expect respect from our children, they deserve equal respect from us when they point out our shortcomings. So when we receive this uncomfortable feedback ("I can't compete with your iPhone"), we have to practice taking a deep breath and saying, "Thanks for letting me know. I'm going to work on that."

Do we always have the patience and wherewithal to respond like this? No, of course not. We are human and imperfect too. And it's normal to feel defensive and think, "I'm the parent," especially if that is the messaging with which we were raised. But parenting is humbling, so we will have lots of chances to practice this attitude shift, and eventually, we can and will do better.

## Phubbing and the Distracted Parent

The scene: You're talking to a friend. Suddenly, your friend's phone pings. Slowly, your friend's eyes drop to the device in their hand, then dart back up as if to reassure you that they are indeed still listening. But it is apparent they are not. Their eyes have glazed over a bit, and you can tell that they're distracted and processing whatever message just crossed their screen. You know you will most likely have to repeat the last few things you said.

Simply put, we cannot multitask when it comes to two activities that require deep thinking and listening. Our friend cannot hear our story and show empathy or concern if they are also trying to read a message that might bring up a different emotional response. This split attention is frustrating for the speaker, who feels unheard, and it is detrimental to the listener, who cannot offer genuine interest or support because of the distraction. This is called phubbing, a mashup of the words *phone* and *snubbing*, and most adults hate this feeling. So it probably won't come as a surprise to hear that children hate it too.

In 2014, the number of mobile devices in the world surpassed the number of people in the world. That same year, University of Michigan professor and pediatrician Jenny Radesky and her research team visited several fast-food restaurants in a shopping mall food court to observe how caregivers interacted with their children.[14] Their research provided an early look at the impact of distracting devices

---

14    Jenny S. Radesky, Caroline J. Kistin, Barry Zuckerman, Katie Nitzberg, Jamie Gross, Margot Kaplan-Sanoff, Marilyn Augustyn, and Michael Silverstein, "Patterns of Mobile Device Use by Caregivers and Children during Meals in Fast Food Restaurants," National Library of Medicine, April 2014, https://pubmed.ncbi.nlm.nih.gov/24616357/.

on relationships: the more they were ignored by their caregivers, who were absorbed in their smartphones, the more the children tried to get their parents' attention, raising their voices, singing, climbing over one another, clambering over the booths or tables, and generally exasperating the adults. This behavior in turn led the caregivers to warn their children multiple times, responding more harshly with each reprimand.

Today, this might be a scene many of us have witnessed or experienced. It's so easy to reach for our phones when we're bored or lonely—such an easy distraction and source of entertainment! And it is so easy to get annoyed when our children interrupt us. As these researchers observed, however, our children are watching.

The good news is that children want and need our attention and they are willing to do a lot to get it. But the bad news is if they can't get us to react to them through positive behavior, children will try to get our attention through negative behavior, like increasing their volume or being obnoxious. So if we're going to address the screentime challenge, we must address our own use of screens before we can meaningfully address our children's.

Our kids learn about what good adulting looks like by watching how we behave, what we do, and, most of all, what we say. They observe us to learn the rules about how to behave in social situations, how to communicate feelings clearly, and how to organize and make plans. So to become tech-intentional, we must look first at our own behaviors regarding screen use. We are, for better or worse, our children's first role models for healthy technology use.

Inevitably, we are going to get some things wrong, but there *are* ways to do a lot of things right. We can learn and implement best practices. We can effectively model balance with technology. And, with the right attitude and strategies, we can reduce conflict. But we must start with ourselves first.

## Parents and Screentime

I know you are trying. I know this is tough. I know I just said to replace judgment with curiosity, and now you may feel judged and defensive. This is *hard*. But we must brave this part of the conversation if we are going to positively change things for our children. Parents who do this work will have greater success implementing long-term solutions.

Here are a few research-backed reasons why we need to look at our own use of screens first: according to Pew Research, 56% of parents feel they spend too much time on their phones, and two-thirds admit to feeling distracted by their devices when they are engaging with their children. Most parents (66%) also believe parenting is harder today than it was for previous generations because of technologies like social media and smartphones.[15]

Another study on the impact of phubbing on parent–child relationships, published in 2021 in the *Journal of Pediatric Nursing* by Susan Solecki, an associate clinical professor of nursing at Drexel University, revealed that 68% of American parents said their smartphones interfered with their ability to spend quality time with their children.[16] So problematic screen use by parents, regardless of their age or education level, adversely affects children. This is a relatively recent phenomenon, so there is no long-term research yet. However, Solecki's research is an early indication that phubbing our children decreases our child's awareness and sensitivity, lowers their verbal and nonverbal communication, and generates problematic behavior. Most importantly, as Radesky's work demonstrates, phubbing interferes with our ability

---

15  Brooke Auxier, Monica Anderson, Andrew Perrin, and Erica Turner, "Parenting Children in the Age of Screens," Pew Research Center, July 28, 2020, https://www.pewresearch.org/internet/2020/07/28/parenting-children-in-the-age-of-screens.

16  Susan Solecki, "The Phubbing Phenomenon: The Impact on Parent-Child Relationships," *Journal of Pediatric Nursing*, 2021.

to connect with our child. Time and time again, research shows that the parent–child relationship is of the greatest importance to healthy child development.

---

## TECH-INTENTIONAL TIPS FOR GROWN-UPS

Addressing our own problematic screen use is a key part of becoming a tech-intentional parent. If we struggle to manage our own device use, then it can't be a surprise that it's hard for our children. Fortunately, there are some simple changes we can make to decrease our scrolling:

- Delete the social media apps from your phone.
- Switch your screen to grayscale.
- Turn off all notifications, including texts.
- Get an alarm clock.
- Keep screens out of the bedroom.
- Be a screentime role model.
- Use books rather than the internet to look up information.
- Replace judgment with curiosity—for yourself!

---

There are other social and emotional reasons why we as parents need to look at our screen use first. Beyond making our children feel bad or behave poorly when our attention is pulled away by our devices, our kids see how much power our devices have over us. From small babies, captivated by the glow of our screens, to the older teens who watch us hypocritically disappear into our devices, they notice. This isn't fair to our children. We may think we have an excellent, justifiable reason to be looking at our phones at any given moment. But from a child's perspective, they only see the backs of our phone cases. They have no idea what we're doing, why we are doing it, or why what we're doing is so much more powerful than what they are asking for or telling us about.

## THE PARENTING QUADRANT

Something else that can get overlooked in the process of becoming tech-intentional is the impact of our own childhood experiences. How we were parented and how we parent often affect the values we hold.

Years ago, I participated in a parenting class with my then-one-year-old son. One day, the instructor introduced something called "The Parenting Quadrant," adapted from the Positive Discipline Association's parenting approach. It mapped out four different parenting styles: the permissive parent, the authoritarian parent, the neglectful parent, and the positive discipline parent.

Until I became a parent, I hadn't really thought about parenting styles. I figured there were some extremes, but for the most part, parenting was parenting. I couldn't have been more wrong, but it took seeing this quadrant for me to realize that there was so much more nuance to being a parent. For example, experiencing parental loss as a child might lead someone to be an anxious parent. Or someone whose parents were their best friends might make it hard to set boundaries as an adult.

As the instructor explained more about the quadrant, I was struck by something: how I was parented influenced how I was parenting. It was, as they say, an aha moment.

### Look Back to Move Forward

Sometimes, to move forward, we must look back. Childhood can be a complex, messy experience. Many of us had parents who tried their best but made mistakes. Some of us had parents who were so in pain from their own bumps and bruises, both literal and figurative, they could not be present for us as children. Sometimes, there was trauma and abuse.

When we become parents, whether we plan for it or not, we bring what we know to the table. Soon enough, our child spills a glass of milk, and the scolding words tumble out of our mouths as we gasp, "I sound like my mother!" We react to our child's misbehaviors the way we were reacted to, whether that was with spanking, empathy, punishment, kindness, shaming, hugging, scolding, time-outs, or yelling. In moments of conflict as parents ourselves, we instinctively go to what we know.

Yes, our childhood took place in a different era. Yes, things have changed. But we carry the experiences of our childhoods into those we provide to our children. Without conscious effort, practice, or therapy, overriding the old habits and hurts of our own experiences is very challenging. Screentime challenges are riddled with conflict and bring out many of our old habits and patterns.

A child's negative behavior regarding screen use feels personal, but we aren't sure why. Their demands and desires to have more and longer time on devices feel like more than the television time we got as children, but it also seems like that's just what kids do today. We can't ask our parents how they navigated social media because it didn't exist 20 years ago. Our screen use is part of our social lives and jobs in a way that our parents' generation never experienced. Therefore, when our children arrive, we know only what we knew— only what was done to us. Even if we read all the parenting books out there, we apply them through the lens of our own lived experience.

## Exercise: Exploring the Parenting Quadrant

To become tech-intentional parents, we have to understand how we were parented. The Parenting Quadrant is a great tool for understanding how our own experience of being parented influenced our parenting approach today. It can also shed light on the different parenting styles between coparents, which can result in numerous disagreements about screentime.

This exercise can bring up a lot of emotions, so be sure to find a time when you feel ready to dive in a little deeper. You can do this either alone or with your parenting partner. Take a look at the following figure.

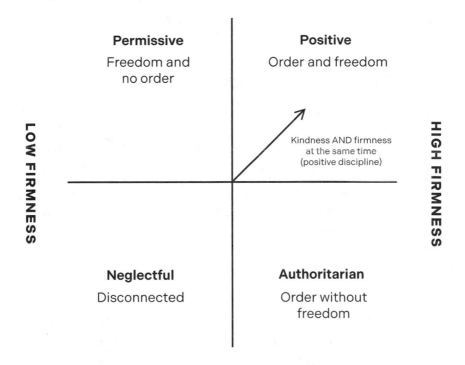

Credit: adapted from Positive Discipline Association, Developing Respectful Boundaries (June 2006)

As you look at the quadrant, consider the following: Where would you place the caregiver(s) you had growing up in terms of parenting style? Were your siblings parented in the same way? Then, consider your parenting style today. Where do you place yourself on this quadrant? If you have a spouse or coparent, where do they fall on this quadrant, how are your parenting styles similar and different, and where might conflict arise?

If you feel ready and able, start the conversation with your coparent, spouse, or another trusted caregiver. Identify where you run into challenges in your own parenting practices. Finally, see if you can have empathy for one another's different experiences; after all, we don't all come to parenting with the same tools.

## Case Study: The Walker Family

When Anna and Jay Walker reached out to me for support, it wasn't just to address their eight-year-old's use of screens; it was to help them prepare for what lay ahead. Many of their peers had children with unlimited access to screens and social media, and they knew they didn't want that for their daughter. Both high-powered executives, these savvy parents knew that more tech was inevitable as their child grew up. They saw the writing on the wall and wanted to get ahead of any issues.

Despite their busy schedules, Anna and Jay made the time in their calendars for our sessions, and they came prepared with thoughtful questions. When we arrived at the session on the Parenting Quadrant, Anna and Jay acknowledged that they had had very different experiences growing up. Anna's parents had been born in another country, and their values were deeply rooted in their culture of origin. While reviewing the Parenting Quadrant, Anna identified that her parents used a high firmness/low kindness style (authoritarian), and she was held to high expectations. Meanwhile, Jay felt that his parents had approached their relationship with their children with high kindness but low firmness (permissive). He and his siblings were friends with their parents, which made it hard for him as a father to say no to his own child.

As a result of these different experiences, the Walkers sometimes experienced conflict when parenting their daughter together. Anna felt that Jay was too lenient on some things, and Jay felt that Anna was too strict. Without judgment, we can see that how Anna and Jay were parented deeply affected their relationship as parents to their own daughter. Identifying these differences was central to moving forward in defining for their daughter—who might one day become a parent herself—how they wanted to parent: a balance of kindness and firmness. Now they could move together toward a common goal.

One important note: parenting isn't linear; it's more like a zigzag. Sometimes we veer too far in one direction (firmness, perhaps) or overcorrect too much in another (e.g., kindness). That's not a bad thing. It's part of the process, and the more we practice, the smoother the line becomes. It won't ever be a straight line, of course. But a tech-intentional parent aims to parent with a good balance of kindness and firmness, even if that path is a little wobbly at times.

## What Children Need

On the Parenting Quadrant, snowplow parents fall into the permissive section: high kindness, low firmness. You might be thinking, *But wait! Is being high in kindness a bad thing?* Rest assured, kindness is not in and of itself bad. Yet kindness without boundaries, limits, or rules—that is, firmness—is actually *unkind*. As Brené Brown famously says, "Clear is kind."[17]

---

17    Brené Brown, *Dare to Lead* (New York, NY: Random House, October 2018).

Similarly, parenting with *only* boundaries and rules (i.e., firmness) is neither healthy nor loving either. Children need both. They need to know they are loved, *and* they need to know what the boundaries are. Children who experience a good dose of both kindness and firmness during their childhoods learn to trust adults and feel safe and secure in their world.

## THE FIGHT WORTH HAVING

Some family conflict is normal. Our children will disagree with some of our parenting choices. The older they get, the more passionately they will fight for their autonomy. The challenge for parents is discerning which battles we want to have. As a parent educator colleague of mine says, "You don't have to attend every fight you are invited to." We can let some things go. Choosing our battles can decrease our stress. But when it comes to setting limits and teaching values around screentime, that is a fight worth having.

When parents contact me, one of the first things they share is how exhausted they are by family conflicts around screens. They are tired of yelling, threatening, fighting, and, ultimately, giving in. They want things to be different, but they don't know what exactly this should look like. They know that screentime affects their child, but they don't know what else to do: the short-term gain feels like the only manageable option, even if the long-term fallout is miserable. And they don't even know where to begin.

Here is where we must start: becoming a tech-intentional parent means fighting for our children's future cognitive, mental, physical, and emotional health. That's the fight worth having. With clearly defined values, an awareness of our own use of screens, and an understanding of our parenting style (and how it was affected by our own childhood experiences), we can go boldly forward.

We will parent in a way that aligns with the values we hold. We will model healthy technology use. And we will use the experiences of our past to fight for our children's future.

Understandably, we will not be perfect all the time. Becoming a tech-intentional parent is a process that takes time, involves mistakes, requires repair, and allows for second chances. But we must remember that we are our children's adult role models: they will behave how we behave. And they will mimic all our choices, including the good, the bad, and the mortifying.

So when it comes to screentime, when we know better, we do better. Achieving a healthy balance with technology use starts with us.

## TL;DR

- Values are the foundation of everything, so start by identifying what matters most to your family.

- Parenting styles impact our parenting. Tech-intentional parents are kind and firm.

- Being tech-intentional means that we fight for our children's future cognitive, mental, physical, and emotional health by how we parent.

# CHAPTER 4

# PUTTING SKILLS BEFORE SCREENS

Babies have an action plan to build their brains healthfully.

—ANNE GREEN GILBERT, FOUNDER OF THE
CREATIVE DANCE CENTER AND BRAINDANCE™

Play is the work of childhood.

—JEAN PIAGET, SWISS PSYCHOLOGIST

**IN THE 1970S, ANNE GREEN GILBERT** was teaching dance to Seattle public school students in their PE classes. At the time, kindergarten students had to demonstrate an ability to skip across the gym to pass into the first grade. But starting around the 1990s, when schools were adding more technology to their programs and replacing movement spaces with computer labs, Gilbert noticed that more than half of her students were unable to skip. But rather than holding those students back a year, which would increase the size of the following year's kindergarten classes, the district simply changed the requirement: children no longer had to demonstrate an ability to skip to graduate from kindergarten.

For many years, the issue of standards has been a hotly debated topic in public education. Policymakers, often with little to no teaching experience themselves, have made decisions about measuring performance to motivate or determine funding for schools. Standards, such as the Common Core, have become the de facto method to evaluate not only student learning but also so-called teacher effectiveness. And because test scores have been increasingly tied to funding, many schools and faculty have shifted their focus to teaching to the test.

Other authors have filled entire books with the many reasons this is deeply problematic. But when we think about the relationship between education and technology use, the key questions become "What skills really matter? And how can we ensure that the skills that do matter for learning and future success aren't being displaced by technology-based skills?" There is a time and a place for technological skills. But children are regularly exposed to technology far before they are developmentally ready.

While writing this book, I reached out to Gilbert and was honored to get her perspective on children, focus, and movement. Back in 1981, Gilbert founded the Creative Dance Center and the Kaleidoscope Dance Company with the intention of training teachers how to incorporate creative dance in a school setting and use all forms of dance in an inclusive, student-centered way. But eventually, just as she had observed with her public school students, Gilbert noticed children arriving at the center less able to focus and pay attention. She could not keep her students engaged for even 30-minute classes. By the late '90s, most of her dance students, not just one or two, exhibited these behaviors. Meanwhile, her fellow school colleagues told her, "We can't teach anymore because of the focus issues." By the 2000s, as the use of screen-based technologies continued to rise, the physical, social, and behavioral problems Gilbert had observed had escalated significantly.

Gilbert knew something serious was happening. Children were becoming more emotionally and behaviorally dysregulated, and it was impacting so many areas of their lives. Increased use of computers in the classroom certainly contributed to this shift, but it wasn't the only factor. Children also spent less time than ever before in movement-based activities, such as unstructured play. Children were somehow missing critical moments of development when they were very young, and it was seriously affecting their ability to focus and learn as they got older.

In response, Gilbert developed a pattern-based approach called BrainDance to help children recenter and regulate their haywire central nervous systems. She saw a positive effect immediately: after just five minutes of performing specific movement patterns at the start of every dance class, her students could suddenly focus for the remaining 25 minutes. Even as technology was creeping more and more into kids' daily activities and impacting their attention spans, Gilbert showed that reorienting their bodies toward physical activity had significant benefits and that movement matters for brain development.

## WE'VE GOT IT BACKWARD

We have decades of research about the skills children need to develop into healthy adults. But we do not yet have long-term research about the impact of excessive screentime, especially at younger ages, on learning and development.

According to a 2017 study released by internet security company AVG Technologies, by age five, more kids knew how to play a computer game or navigate a smartphone than tie their shoes. Today, parents download apps to help children read by age four, teach coding skills to prepare them for tech-based careers, and provide smartphones and social media to connect tweens to their friends.

At the same time, parents are bombarded with headlines about how children are falling behind academically, how tech skills are imperative for future success, and how we are failing as parents if we don't provide tech early and often. And, of course, we receive all this information via alerts, notifications, and feeds on our own personal devices. But no tech-based tools will prove beneficial unless (and until) we prioritize certain skills first.

Kindergarten has changed dramatically in the past generation. Classrooms that used to be about learning and skill building through dress-up corners, play kitchens, and book nooks are now filled with individual desks and chairs, reading levels, and sight words. In elementary school, digital tablets are used for math and science curricula. And rather than enjoying an old-school pizza party, elementary students who have achieved a classroom goal are rewarded with "device days," when they are allowed to bring personal devices, such as tablets or smartphones, to school as a celebration (a concept that yields numerous problems, particularly around equity since not all children have devices). Middle and high school look really different too. Paper planners and textbooks have been replaced with learning management systems and eBooks. Extracurricular programs and athletics use social media sites to communicate and share information.

But assigning reading at younger ages and displacing paper planners with online versions are not in a child's best developmental interests. Young children's visual systems are not yet fully developed and integrated. Play and movement develop the skills children need to learn how to read. Some countries understand this. In Finland, for example, children don't begin school until they are seven years old, yet they often score high on international reading tests. But in other countries, such as the United States, teaching reading is now occurring at younger and younger ages even though this runs counter to how children develop literacy.

Beyond brain development, the effects of children spending more time on screens and less time in movement are growing more pronounced when it comes to their physical development. For example, optometrists reported that excessive tech use during the pandemic accelerated vision problems in children, including myopia, or nearsightedness, which causes difficulty in seeing farther distances clearly. Interestingly, while there is currently no cure for myopia, there is some emerging evidence that spending time outdoors—rather than focusing on screens indoors all day—might delay or prevent it.

Other physical problems can occur when we put screen use before skill development. The posture of tweens and teens, stooped for hours over their devices for years, becomes shockingly apparent when they cross the stage at graduation. Our pediatrician said that he has seen more cases of scoliosis in his exam room than ever before because of kids spending their days and evenings hunched over screens and moving less. Children and adults alike have developed neck pain, or so-called tech neck, and even bone spurs because of strained posture from holding phones and spending time glued to screens.

All of these symptoms of excessive tech use make it clear: we have things backward.

Although some skills *can* be taught on screens, children do not *need* screens to build most skill sets. Instead, children need to develop certain skills *before* they have access to screens. We need to realign the experience of childhood with child development. We need to reverse the order so that we expose children to analog before digital skills. We need to reprioritize what we focus on when our children are still young and developing before we toss them the tablets and smartphones.

Technology can come eventually, but it cannot come at the expense of the skills children need to grow into healthy, well-rounded adults. In fact, according to recent research by multiple organizations, such as the McKinsey Global Institute, while the need for technological skills in future careers will continue to grow, so will social, emotional, and higher cognitive skills, such as critical thinking, creativity, flexibility, and empathy. We cannot forgo the latter for the sake of the former.

We actually shouldn't want our kids to walk before they crawl or read before they skip. As Anne Green-Gilbert witnessed, the cross-lateral movements of crawling and skipping build brain connections. In her book *The Hidden Link Between Vision and Learning*, Wendy Rosen discusses how crawling and walking are foundational to visual development, and therefore, to learning.[18] A child must learn to skip before they can read. Moving through these patterns with ease is an indicator that reflexes are integrated and binocular vision is in place—both necessary developmental steps. Only when we've mastered the first skill can we begin to learn the next. So why are parents downloading apps to teach toddlers to read or offering supposedly educational games before children start formal schooling? Why do schools expect tweens and teens to use tech-based tools to manage their learning experiences before they've developed the brain functions to be able to effectively do so? Why do we assume that staying socially connected to friends requires social media and smartphones?

A child who follows typical developmental patterns is said to be neurotypical. A child who doesn't exhibit the typical developmental trajectory is neurodiverse. But parents are left to their own devices, literally and figuratively, when it comes to understanding child development in general and their own children specifically. When parents

---

18    Wendy Rosen, *The Hidden Link Between Vision and Learning* (Washington, DC: Rowman & Littlefield, 2016).

have a basic understanding of what neurotypical child development looks like, however, we can better understand our child's responses to different experiences. For example, consider the relationship between development and temperament: development refers to the stages of growth that a child goes through, whereas temperament comprises the behavioral traits that each child exhibits that affect how they approach the world. Our child's temperament impacts how they develop. So biological siblings can be complete opposites in personality and how they respond behaviorally to situations, such as screentime.

As we strive to be tech-intentional parents, we must consider our children's development and temperament when deciding how to set appropriate limits. There are some in my field who will argue for zero screentime for children, even into their teen years, but I do not believe that is a practical approach in today's reality—though I certainly champion anyone's efforts to try! At some point, children *will* be introduced to screen-based technology, whether at home, through peers, or at school; the how and the when will vary considerably.[19] And for most children and families, screens are very much embedded in our culture and lives. So the best approach to protecting our children and setting them up for future success lies in prioritizing key areas of development *before* the deluge of screentime so that when the flood arrives, they will at least be better prepared.

## PIAGET'S FOUR STAGES OF CHILD DEVELOPMENT[20]

Piling up the preflood sandbags starts with improving our parental understanding of how children typically develop. Swiss psychologist

---

19  Not all screentime in school is bad. See Everyschool.org for an excellent breakdown of the types of screentime.

20  See Appendix B for a chart describing Piaget's developmental stages and corresponding recommendations by the World Health Organization and the American Academy of Pediatrics.

Jean Piaget is best known for his theory of neurotypical child development, which he splits into four stages: sensorimotor, pre-operational, concrete operational, and formal operational. I find these categories helpful in understanding development at different ages: infancy, preschool and early childhood, later childhood, and adolescence.

Here are my brief summaries of each of Piaget's four stages:

1. **Sensorimotor** (birth to two years old): In this stage, babies learn about their world through movement and touch. Children see themselves as separate beings from other people and objects. They learn that their actions can cause things to happen and about object permanence, which is the belief that things still exist even when they go away, like a parent leaving the room. Through their interactions with caregivers, they develop early language skills.

2. **Preoperational** (two to seven years old): In this stage, young children learn that words and pictures can represent objects, which is called symbolic thinking. They are egocentric, finding it difficult to take the perspective of others (think "threenagers"). Very concrete thinkers, they struggle with logic and point of view, which makes the concept of sharing difficult at this age because they do not understand the significance or importance of this skill. Language development emerges.

3. **Concrete operational** (seven to eleven years old): In this stage, children's thinking grows more logical and organized, though it is still quite concrete. They start to use reasoning (i.e., inductive logic) to make sense of the world, and they are getting better at understanding other people's points of view. This age group struggles with abstract and hypothetical concepts.

4. **Formal operational** (adolescence to adulthood): In this final stage, abstract thinking develops. Tweens and teens can reason about hypothetical situations and have thoughts about moral or philosophical issues. They use deductive reasoning and can see multiple potential solutions to a problem. They can plan for the future.

Piaget's four stages represent neurotypical child development. New levels of comprehension unfold and build on previously learned knowledge. This flow of neurotypical development makes sense. Our interruption of this flow through the introduction of screens too early or too often, however, interferes with this logical unfolding. Babies cannot walk before they learn to crawl. Tweens cannot manage social media toxicity until they develop perspective taking—and even then, online toxicity can still be painful, to which many adults can attest (and their brains are fully developed!).

## EXCEPTIONS TO SCREENTIME LIMITS

Many children are neurodiverse, and these children may have needs that require the use of technology. For example, when it comes to screens and development, students with certain learning disabilities (e.g., nonverbal autism or dyslexia) can use tech-based tools to communicate. A child with diabetes may use a smart device to monitor glucose levels. A marginalized or otherwise ostracized child, such as a transgender student in a school or geographic area where there are hostile views or even potential physical threats toward gender-diverse children, may find support and resources in an online community. These are intentional uses of technology that are life changing for certain children and therefore clear exceptions to the skills-before-screens rule. For these children, the screen serves as a tool for developing a skill or providing a support network that may not be available in the analog world. This book is *not* about that subset of children, and I defer to other experts on that.

Some educators and even clinicians argue that screen-based devices are useful for neurological differences such as attention deficit hyperactivity disorder (ADHD). One school principal told me that allowing her middle school students to have personal devices actually helped with their ADHD. I do not yet feel fully convinced myself that the potential positive effects of screens outweigh the numerous risks, especially for children with impulse-control challenges, though there is emerging evidence-based research to support my view on this topic. As with so many things, it depends—on the medium, the child, the school, and the developmental stage. Technology can be a remarkable tool when used intentionally, in alignment with values, and at the appropriate developmental pace and level of the user. Unfortunately, most screen-based technologies today, especially those in school, rarely meet those criteria.

We don't learn to read before we know our *ABC*s; we don't write books until we have mastered five-paragraph essays; we don't join the varsity team until we learn to dribble and pass. There are steps in developmental processes that cannot be overlooked, and if we go out of order, we miss out on key building blocks that matter significantly in the future. Then, as Gilbert noticed in her dancers, when that unstable foundation starts to wobble, we wonder where things went wrong.

## THE SKILLS OUR KIDS *DO* NEED

When it comes to realigning childhood with child development, a tech-intentional parent will prioritize three things: executive function skills, movement and play, and empathy and compassion.

## Skill #1: Executive Function Skills

Executive function skills are fundamental to human development. These cognitive abilities are housed in the prefrontal cortex, the very last part of our brain to fully develop (i.e., not until we are in our 20s or 30s!). Regardless of our developmental path, neurotypical or neurodiverse, we all use executive function skills daily. These skills include time management, organization, planning, prioritizing, cognitive flexibility, metacognition, focus, impulse control, and emotion regulation—which are pretty important across all areas of our lives!

We often hear executive function discussed in the context of an ADHD diagnosis. With ADHD, executive function is impaired in some way, though it can look very different from one person to another. For example, someone with ADHD might struggle with being on time (time management), completing a project (planning), or struggling to pay attention in class (focus). A neurodiverse way of thinking and seeing the world makes for a much more interesting classroom or family, and I see it as a superpower.

The unfortunate reality, however, is that most schools—and most workplaces and some households—do not see it like this, nor do they build their systems to embrace and support neurological differences. Often, a child's environment does not address neurodiverse ways of learning that might be beneficial for that child but instead contributes to or exacerbates the symptoms of ADHD. And those symptoms of ADHD are similar to those of excessive screentime use: when children are engaged in screen-based technology that is designed to hook and hold their attention, regulating emotion or maintaining focus—both indicators of ADHD—becomes even more challenging. I can't help but wonder whether ADHD diagnoses have increased partly because screentime has increased. I believe clinicians and parents need to explore the screentime angle anytime they are seeking an ADHD diagnosis or treatment.

All of us use executive function skills in the tasks we do, and we start building them from the moment we are born. Executive function skills aren't typically taught in isolation but in conjunction with other skills, such as eye tracking, large motor skills, reading, getting to class on time, social interactions, or finishing a work project. Some schools have realized their importance and offer study skills or learning support classes to help students improve their executive function skills. However, we have a lot more work to do, especially as children are increasingly being required to use screens for school, which paradoxically interferes with executive function because it means requiring neurodiverse children to spend more time on platforms that negatively impact their ability to stay on task or manage their time.

## Skill #2: Movement and Play

Playing on screens is not the same as playing with friends and toys in the real world. Anne Green Gilbert understood this when she developed BrainDance, incorporating playful movements to help children improve their focus, attention, and lifelong learning.

In his studies of development, Piaget said, "Play is the work of childhood." But adults often discount play as important or facilitating real learning because we see play as the reward we get for working hard. For children, that's not the case at all. Play *is* their work, and we need to give them as much time and opportunity to practice it as possible.

Parents help their children build strong executive function by prioritizing play. This may seem easier when our children are young, but play is still very important to older kids too; it just might look different and might not be called "play." It can include throwing around a ball outside with parents, peers, or pets; participating in pick-up games or organized individual and team sports; performing in a band; putting together puzzles; or playing board games.

Too often, schools and parents cut play short by shortening recess or denying access to unstructured play, but executive function and empathy-building skills get practiced and strengthened in physical activity and play. Children need time to learn to connect with one another in the real world. Children won't develop these skills by spending time isolated online or playing video or social media games in the digital one.

The more we practice a skill, the stronger it becomes. When parents understand the benefits of real-world play to development, we see how screen-based play does *not* provide the same opportunities to build skills as do real-life interactions with other children.

## Skill #3: Empathy and Compassion

Research shows that when children develop skills like empathy and compassion, they are further strengthening executive function. But there is growing concern that excessive use of social media platforms, especially as brains are maturing, can decrease empathy toward others. Social media companies have admitted that they can't filter everything (and their efforts are weak at best, as Facebook whistleblower Frances Haugen revealed in 2021), and their algorithms push toxic content within minutes of logging on (e.g., the Center for Countering Digital Hate reported that 13-year-olds were seeing recommended content about eating disorders and self-harm within half an hour of joining TikTok). It is far easier to be mean behind the screen than it is to say something cruel to a friend's face. Comment threads across the internet are full of trolls hiding behind keyboards and flinging anger and hatred at others from the comfort of their own homes. Even adults, with fully formed brains, are hardly immune to the pain of social media toxicity or comment thread vitriol.

Children who seem like the kindest, sweetest children in the real world participate in this online cruelty, which comes as a shock to their teachers and parents. This is because when young children first interact with others online, their executive function is still growing and developing. Facial expressions, social cues, sarcasm, emotion regulation, and more are all new pieces of information to absorb while they work to make friends and identify allies. The isolation of the pandemic also decreased the opportunity to practice social skills with other children in person. Following a return to the classroom, teachers observed a decline in skills such as perspective taking and empathy, reporting that while children might be physically two years older, their social and emotional skills seemed stuck in prepandemic stages of development. Although children are fully capable of rebuilding these skills eventually, the delays can further complicate a parent's decision about when to introduce smartphones and social media. Not only are many children not developmentally ready, but they may actually be a couple of years behind in maturity too.

When we're face-to-face with our peers, we get immediate feedback; when we're cruel online, we don't get social cues that tell us we went too far. No parent wants to believe their kid is capable of cruelty to others, but the unfortunate reality is that people feel much safer being mean online; it's a well-known-enough phenomenon that researchers have named it the online disinhibition effect. This aligns with where children are developmentally: they are more impulsive and less likely to think about the consequences of their actions. They lack the ability to take another's viewpoint.

Unfortunately, there are horrifying examples of online cruelty leading to self-harm and even suicide. One teacher shared with me a tragic story of a high school student who was watching pornography—on a school-issued device, no less—and masturbating in a school bathroom stall. Another student recorded the act, then shared the video with the entire student body. Within seconds, the whole school knew what had occurred. That evening, the humiliated student committed suicide. When young people are handed the power of technology at the same time as they are building critical skills, tragedies like this can occur.

Another parent shared with me a story about her son's role in the state championship basketball game. He played for a big high school, where sports were an important part of a student's identity and achievement. The game had been close. Now, in the final few seconds, the score was tied, and this young man had an opportunity to make a game-winning shot . . . and he missed. Game over. Heartbroken and feeling responsible for his team's loss, he later logged onto his social media account as a distraction. Within a few hours of the loss, he had over 500,000—half a million!—comments on his Instagram page, berating him for the error.

Building empathy comes from face-to-face relationships, practicing skills, making mistakes, and seeing the whole person. How many of these negative comments were from people who didn't even know him? And regarding those who did, it's much harder to be mean to someone in your class when you know a little more about who they are. When we make assumptions, we *other* people: we find things to dislike about them, then look for examples of those things, which we turn into validation of our reasons for disliking them in the first place. And for some students in marginalized communities, such as individuals who identify as gender diverse, important support exists online, but the same need for caution still applies because those communities are also more frequently targeted by online hate and cruelty.

Technology companies know that mean stuff gets clicks. The algorithms therefore make this negative content more visible, searchable, and frequent. Children (and adults) will continue to click, share, and comment. It's a vicious cycle.

## THE PROBLEM WITH SCREENS BEFORE SKILLS

Screentime interferes with neurotypical child development, particularly impacting executive function, movement and play, and empathy and compassion. One of the hardest parts about parenting around screentime is when it is time for screentime to be over. So many parents dread the reaction they know they are going to get. There are several reasons why this interaction can be so unpleasant, but a child's development is an important piece to understanding this struggle. Piaget's stages can be a useful guide for parents in understanding how and why a child reacts to screentime the way they do.

For very young children in the sensorimotor stage (birth to two years old), learning starts through communicating with caregivers through sounds, touch, and movement. When we are distracted by a personal device or they are left to be entertained by a screen, their movement and early language skills aren't developing in the way they need—but such skills build healthy brain connections. Although an infant won't necessarily express displeasure like a toddler, they will definitely let us know that they want our attention and may grab at our phone to hold and touch it ("if Mom or Dad likes this, then I like it too") or swat it away from us to redirect our focus back to them. A child makes regular bids for our love and focus. Screens interfere with that.

In the preoperational stage, young children (two to seven years old) don't yet know how to take another person's perspective. They can't see why it is important to someone else, such as their parents, that they stop screentime. They see it very egocentrically: "Stopping screentime impacts me, and I don't like it!" Because they are still building skills in language and emotion, their displeasure might be expressed by shouting, hitting, yelling, or throwing a tantrum because that is how they express their feelings at this age. As parents of these young children, we must not let our own emotional response prevent us from providing the support our child needs. This is very challenging; parents need and deserve breaks to protect their own mental health. But our children learn about emotion regulation by watching how we handle stress and frustration, so we must model that behavior.

The early tweenagers of the concrete operational stage (ages seven through eleven) may understand *logically* that screentime is over but lack the emotion regulation and impulse control to actually stop when asked. They may start to negotiate or bargain with parents to get more screentime. They may argue that "this level isn't over" or "I'm almost done with this episode" to prolong their time. They might better understand our frustrations about ending screentime than younger children do, but at the same time, their need for social approval is increasing, and their peers are increasingly getting their first devices.

Finally, the formal operational stage of development (adolescence to adulthood) is when children begin to understand *why* limit setting around screentime might be beneficial for their health, focus, and relationships. That doesn't mean they will stop completely or willingly, but this age group can understand the potential ethical, moral, and philosophical reasons to balance screen use with other activities. They might see that excessive social media use is impacting their grades or that having their phone out while they study is distracting. Even as their awareness increases, however, it's important to note that this stage extends into early adulthood and that teens especially still need a lot of support and tools to find balance with screens.

All children need off-screen opportunities to build skills, move their bodies, play with friends, and develop empathy and compassion. Fortunately, there are several things parents can do to prioritize these skills before screens.

## SOLUTIONS

Children's needs and abilities vary. Our job as parents is to provide ample opportunities to build skills throughout childhood so that when screentime is introduced, our children have a strong foundation to fall back on. I'm under no illusions that screentime can be introduced without issue; it would be irresponsible for me to suggest otherwise. There isn't really any safe way for children to use social media or the internet unsupervised. But to adapt Douglas Gentile's theory of the displacement effect, parents can take steps to displace screentime in favor of skill-building.

The following are three solutions to prioritize skill building. Think of them as the three *P*s: planners, play, and parents.

### The Planner

Take the humble planner. When I was a middle school teacher, I encouraged my students to track and plan their various homework assignments. Every class period, we would spend the first few minutes writing down their upcoming work and talking about how to manage a longer-term project versus nightly homework assignments.

Today, despite my best efforts to implement the planner, my own teen comes home from school with his laptop, on which he opens a learning management system to find out whatever homework assignments he has for the evening. Within these kinds of platforms, teachers have several locations to post assignments, so children (and frustrated parents) are left to hunt and peck for what they need to know to complete homework. This seems a colossal waste of time and energy and could be avoided by having our kids simply open a paper planner and, in a matter of seconds, see what they wrote down earlier in the day.

For many children in middle school—and certainly for those with executive function skill challenges (e.g., ADHD)—there can be a tendency to think of time-bound tasks as a binary *now* or *not now*. The goal in teaching executive function skills with a planner is not to annoy them into writing things down but rather to help students map out the various steps that will take them from *not now* to *a little bit each day until the deadline* and to see the process that unfolds from the first task until the last. For future work responsibilities, this is a vital skill: tweens and teens can learn how to complete projects and tasks on deadline by pacing their work and breaking things down into smaller chunks.

When we ask students to rely on digital management tools, as is increasingly happening in schools, we displace the opportunity to build these executive function skills first. It isn't that management tools aren't helpful later, but they cannot come until the initial skills have been strengthened and practiced.

As parents, we have more power than we realize. There are things we can do to protect our children's development and prioritize exposure to nontechnological skill-building experiences that truly matter for future success

## When "I'm Bored" Means "I Want Screentime"

When our children say they are bored, our common response is to hand over a screen. Unfortunately, screentime will kill boredom, but it will also kill creativity. Yes, I know kids can be creative online. But studies have shown that only a small percentage of the time children spend on screens is in creative pursuits; mostly, they're consuming passively (e.g., watching videos and scrolling), not writing the next great novel or coding a program.

And as screen use has increased and their time spent in free play has decreased, children haven't flexed their play-based muscles. They might not know how to play in real life when screentime ends.

Parents who want to reduce screentime in their homes have to reframe their thinking around boredom. We need to see it as an opportunity, not a crisis, and teach our kids to see it that way too. We also need to help them learn or remember how to play. And playing on a screen is very different from real-world play.

For example, playing Minecraft is not the same thing as building with wooden blocks. In terms of brain development, building with 3D blocks in the real world is very different from manipulating 2D blocks on a screen. But I can understand why parents are confused about Minecraft. It was developed in 2011 by Mojang Studios and today has more than 141 million monthly active users. It is a wildly popular sandbox game, meaning it allows players a certain degree of freedom to play, build, and explore within the game. I don't fundamentally object to Minecraft. It is a game that my own children have enjoyed. However, like many other digital games, it has no true ending. So when it comes time to turn off the device or power down the console, children are likely to engage in meltdowns and exhibit emotional dysregulation.

Children need opportunities to play off screen so that they can build the skills that eventually will help them build emotion regulation and perspective taking. When it comes to tactile, hands-on play, here are some ideas.

**For littles, play might look like this:**

- Taking all the items out of the recycling bin to build a rocket ship

- Narrating an imaginary game out loud, losing themselves in an imaginative world adults cannot see

- Engaging in messy, tactile artwork, such as painting, Play-Doh, and chalk (sensory-based play for young children is wonderful for brain development)

- Working together with other children to organize a game

- Negotiating, debating, and compromising with peers

- Dancing, singing, and moving

**For middles, play might look like this:**

- Playing an instrument alone or with peers

- Spending time with friends in a variety of environments

- Playing on a team, learning sportsmanship and leadership skills

- Expressing creativity through drama, dance, writing, or art

- Learning how to navigate social relationships and feelings through gentle and consensual teasing

All children need opportunities for play. Play builds healthy brains. Screentime should never displace or replace opportunities for unstructured play. Especially following the isolation and stress of the global pandemic, children more than ever need a way to process their feelings, practice their social skills, and build their executive function. Play is a free, easy way to do that.

## Three Key Questions to Ask Before Handing Our Child a Screen

We often give children screentime when we need time to do something for ourselves. Even as a tech-intentional parent, there will still be moments when giving or allowing screentime buys a moment of sanity or a chance to get something done. That's okay. The difference will be that we are choosing those moments *intentionally*.

We can get to intentionality by asking ourselves three key questions before handing our child a screen:

1. **When we choose a screen-based option, what do we gain?** For most parents, the most common answer is "convenience" or "time." We need to get something done, immediately, and we know the screens will occupy their attention. Occasionally, this is fine. But it's a slippery slope when screentime becomes our go-to habit. We want to keep it the exception, not the rule.

2. **When we choose a screen-based option, what do we lose or replace?** This is the hard one because we know that even if in the short term, we buy ourselves 20 minutes, when it's time to turn off the screens, we are going to see a meltdown or a fight. And because we're so worn down already, we give in, which continues this tricky cycle and ultimately only makes things harder. When it comes to what we replace, we must think about what is *not* happening when our kids are spending time on screens. Are they reading, playing with friends (off screen), doing homework, helping around the house, being bored, or going outside? We know what children need, and what they need isn't on a screen.

3. **Finally, when we choose a screen-based option, what do we model?** I know that when we as adults are bored, we pull out our phones and scroll. Children watch and learn by observing us. They learn that boredom is a bad thing to be avoided rather than a source of creativity. There are upsides to digital technology and what it allows us to do in the world. But it is our job as parents to model how we cope with boredom or downtime so our children see us making choices about when to pull out our devices.

The solution isn't doing *no* screentime; it's being intentional about the screentime we do have. And if we start this when our children are young, it's much easier to enforce when our children are older.

## NOT ALL HOPE IS LOST

Brains can and do adapt. The younger the brain, the easier and more quickly it can change. But as experts such as psychiatrist Norman Doidge, author of *The Brain That Changes Itself*, have found, even older individuals who have experienced strokes can recover with effort and attention to repatterning neural pathways.[21]

For children who've been exposed to excessive screentime or who seem deeply impacted by even small amounts, there is always an opportunity to make even small changes. There is also work. Change depends on the depth of the damage and the effort and commitment of the caregivers. We also must parent the model we got, not the one we wish we had.

Returning to what we know about how children learn best, Piaget's stages of development, and the decades of research that exist to support them, we can prioritize the experiences that build healthy brains: time outside, physical activity, and in-person interaction with other children. All of these contribute to the development of executive function, play and movement, and empathy and compassion—and these are the skills that truly matter.

At the end of my interview with Anne Green Gilbert, I asked if she had hope for the future of children. "I've never doubted this work," she replied. "I know it works. I see it—the importance of movement. I don't doubt it." She paused. "But I also don't go on the internet."

---

21  Norman Doidge, MD, *The Brain That Changes Itself* (New York: Penguin, December 2017).

## TL;DR

- We must focus on helping our children develop the skills that matter: executive function, movement and play, and empathy and compassion.

- No two children are alike; we must adjust our parenting expectations accordingly.

- Prioritize play; it is the work of childhood.

- When we do choose screentime, remember to ask the three key questions: What do we gain, what do we lose or replace, and what do we model?

CHAPTER 5

# IT STARTS WITH US: BUILDING AWARENESS OF PARENTAL SCREEN USE

When my mom is on her phone, she is so distracted,
I can do anything. I asked her for $500 the other day,
and she said yes, but later, she didn't even remember.

—MY FORMER SEVENTH-GRADE STUDENT

**YEARS AGO, I WORKED** at a center specializing in supporting individuals with ADHD. Most of my clients were middle schoolers, who were in their prime years of executive function development. As we explored in the previous chapter, executive function skills are foundational to future learning and a successful adulthood, and we are increasingly aware that excessive screentime can interfere with healthy development.

While there are many expert opinions about how to treat and respond to ADHD, one of my colleagues at the center used a unique strategy to teach children to build executive function skills. She encouraged them to "live their lives out loud." For children with ADHD, this meant saying aloud what they were doing in their homework assignments, chores, and responsibilities. Articulating their activities brought attention to the steps necessary to complete their tasks and also highlighted the skills they were building. As a child sat down to do homework, for example, they might say, "I'm pulling out my binder and getting a pencil. Then, I need to get my math book out. The first thing I need to do is read the directions." (I know most students today are pulling out tablets or laptops to do their homework, but I cling to the hope that a few are still using paper and pencil and printed textbooks.)

Because executive function challenges can interfere with time management and organization, this approach helped students draw their focus to the task at hand. Additionally, verbalizing these steps used a different part of their brains and broke down the tasks into smaller, more manageable tasks. By using a strategy like this to help strengthen their executive function skills, these clients learned more about not only how their brains worked but also what they could do to increase their focus and task completion.

As I worked with my young clients on building their executive function skills, many parents also expressed concerns about their child's desire to use or play on screens for entertainment and socialization. At the same time, these children were increasingly required to use technology for their school lessons and homework assignments. To help these children, I found that much of our session was spent hunting through online learning management systems to find homework assignments or toggling between tabs to help them organize their essays.

It struck me that if the bulk of our time together was filled with this ineffective approach that did nothing to strengthen executive function skills and these tech-based tools made focusing on a single task incredibly difficult—not just for these children but for myself as well—we weren't helping anyone. If my client's parents were already concerned about screen use outside of school *and* screen use for school was increasing, I couldn't see how these online tools were benefiting students who were already struggling to focus or organize in the first place.

It was another lightbulb moment. After several months of working with these students, two thoughts occurred to me: First, the symptoms of ADHD looked a lot like the symptoms of screen addiction, so we needed to be asking families about screentime in their home. And second, the strategy of living our lives out loud to build clients' executive function skills could also be applied to how we used screens—not just for my young clients but for their parents as well.

## ALL KIDS HAVE SCREENTIME— EVEN THE ONES WHO DON'T

Screentime can mean a lot of different things. It's not just our phones or computers; it includes the smart devices in our homes (e.g., refrigerators and doorbells), our cars (e.g., GPS), the registers at the grocery store, the menus and check-out devices at restaurants, and the digital check-in counters at airports. So when parents today tell me, "My child doesn't get any screentime," I recognize that there are very few families for whom this is true. For example, one such family I know lives in a rural area, homeschools their children, and because one of their children is immunosuppressed, they have very little contact with the outside world. They are truly an exception to the rule—but the children certainly know what a computer and smartphone are, and their parents both use phones and the internet.

Parents who believe their children aren't using tech aren't being dishonest. They are trying to do what they think is best. But what they mean is "I don't give my child a tablet *to entertain them.*" There is a subtle implication here: that this is a choice that all parents could make if they wanted to.

This reaction is reflected in the school surveys I conduct. Parents of younger children sometimes describe parents of older children who have devices as simply bad parents. There is judgment in assumption. But remember: judgment serves no one. A family who says their children are screen free is just a family who hasn't yet been inundated by the increasingly technology-based world we inhabit or had an iPad thrust at them by their school district. It is only a matter of time.

Some parents let their children get smartphones when they are eight years old. Other parents delay until eighth grade. Some parents let kids watch a show while they make dinner. Others limit all screentime except for weekly family movies. Some parents trust their children to figure things out. Others rely on parental controls to monitor.

What individual parents have decided to do about screentime up until this point doesn't actually matter; the *impact* on children does. Being sanctimonious about parenting choices, being blinded by our own privilege, or assuming we've figured it out before our children hit middle school doesn't eliminate the future reality that all children will be exposed, in one way or another, to screen-based technology at some point.

Why is this exposure inevitable? Despite best intentions, if any adult around a child is using a screen, that child is having screentime, even if they aren't looking directly at it. The minute children enter middle school—public, charter, or private—with very few exceptions, screen-based platforms will be a part of their educational experience. Their peers, whose families may hold different values about screen use, will have smartwatches, smartphones, and, eventually, social media and will use it around other children. Pop culture is inundated by and reflective of digital tech. Screen-based technology is inescapable in the modern world.

I know someone who lives without a phone (smart or dumb). He has no internet at home and no email address. He uses pay phones to call me, writes on a computer that is not connected to the internet, and delivers me handwritten memos instead of emails. But his life is increasingly difficult. Parking meters don't take coins. There are fewer and fewer pay phones available. People ask him all the time why he doesn't use email. So we can try to emulate this type of existence, delaying and even denying access to devices for our children for as long as possible. To some extent, that is a family choice. Yet the world has shifted dramatically to being tech reliant, whether we like it or not, and it will become increasingly more difficult to go without or say no completely.

In a way, technology use is like secondhand smoke: children may not be holding the cigarette, but they are watching us smoke and breathing in our air. Similarly, when we hold our phones or scroll on our computers, our children are learning when we use devices, why we use tech (if we tell them), how it might make us feel (if we express it), and how compelling our devices are to us. They see that where our attention goes is where our energy flows. They learn that if they interrupt us, we will get frustrated or mad.

When our children are younger, we tend to think about screen-time rules and contracts as something we will deal with later. But reality is quickly catching up: children are being exposed to screen-based technologies earlier and earlier.

## CHILDREN ARE GETTING SCREENTIME IF . . .

To become tech-intentional and to be able to live our lives out loud, we first need to broaden our view of screentime. Children have multiple ways to access screentime, even before it is formally offered.

**Before children are born:**

- Their parents use pregnancy apps to monitor growth

- Their gender is revealed in a party or celebration, with videos or photos posted online

- Their parents post ultrasound pictures on social media

- They are assigned a social media handle or email address with their name (yes, some parents do this before their children are born)

**Infancy:**

- Video chats with relatives

- Photos or videos of the baby online, such as on social media

- Birth announcements sent via email or social media

- Stats (e.g., weight, height, and growth) posted online

- Apps that track sleep, feeding, or diapering

- Caregivers who use devices around the infant

- Devices used to distract a baby while diapering

- Devices to occupy a baby's attention in the car

- Tech-based tools to soothe, comfort, or monitor breathing or sleeping

## Toddler:

- Playing "educational" apps and games

- Watching shows or streaming content

- Watching YouTube or YouTube Kids

- Listening to audio (e.g., music, podcasts, stories, or sleep meditations) using digital devices

- Being given technology by childcare centers or providers to be entertained (e.g., videos), given physical breaks (e.g., Class Dojo), or distracted (e.g., apps)

- Using devices while waiting (e.g., at a sibling's soccer game, in line at the grocery store, or in the car during traffic)

- Having sleep or meals monitored via apps used by caregivers

- Seeing social media influencers (e.g., a three-year-old TikTok star)

- Having photos and videos publicly posted (i.e., "sharenting"), sometimes even to be shamed, embarrassed, or humiliated, and/or available for download by strangers

## Elementary school:

- Peer pressure to play popular games or use social media (e.g., Roblox, Minecraft, YouTube, or TikTok)

- Smartwatches and smartphones

- Smartphone or smartwatch use by peers on the school bus, on the playground, or during free time

- Use of platforms that collect data (e.g., YouTube Kids knows what videos are viewed and how often), push content, and implement algorithms that create marketing profiles of young children

- In-class apps (e.g., Typing Ninja or Prodigy)

- In-class platforms (e.g., Seesaw, Schoology, or Canvas)

- In-class digital curricula and gamification (i.e., turning schoolwork into games to make them more engaging)

- Elementary schools without "away for the day" policies

- Tech time or device day at school as a reward for good behavior or grades

**Middle and high school:**

- Peers on the bus with their own devices

- Smartphones or smartwatches in the classroom

- Digital tools for school and sanctioned or required by the school

- Online grading platforms

- Finding ways around the rules (e.g., using Google Docs to chat in class)

- Photos or videos being posted or taken without permission

- Social media (including posts about mental health and stress)

- Texting with friends

- After-school activities or sports being communicated via social media platforms

- Cyberbullying through apps and social media

- Sexting and sextortion through apps and social media

- Financial tools online (e.g., credit cards, Apple Pay, Venmo, or PayPal)

This is by no means an exhaustive list, and there will always be new items to add. Children will be exposed to something tech based at some point in their childhood. The hope is that they are introduced to it in ways that are developmentally appropriate and emphasize skills and safety, in alignment with family values.

## LIVING OUR LIVES OUT LOUD

Whether we like it or not, our children learn about technology use by watching us first. And we have work to do—no question. We are on our phones more than we'd like or should be, and we are blurring work, social life, scrolling, and family time. These challenges are not our fault, but it is our responsibility to address them. So when my colleague at the ADHD center taught me about living our lives out loud, I knew this was an idea that could easily be applied to how we talk about and address screen use.

Living our life out loud around technology means narrating what we do as we do it any time we are using, reaching for, touching, or reacting to a digital tool. We strive to do this *every* time about *everything* we do on screens, even when it's mundane and boring.

There are layers to this process. First, we start with just stating the facts about what we are doing. Some examples might sound like this:

- "I'm reaching for my phone to text Dad to find out what time he's coming home."

- "I'm going to go look up a recipe on my phone."

- "I need to see when your music lesson is on the calendar."

- "I'm checking the weather to see if we need raincoats."

Then, we might add another element of describing how these actions are making us feel or naming the experiences we are having while we are using or reaching for our devices:

- "I feel bored. I'm reaching for my phone."

- "These notifications interrupt me all the time. It makes it hard for me to focus."

- "I thought looking at my friend's social media page would make me feel better. It didn't."

- "I was only picking up my phone to look at the time, but suddenly I'm scrolling through the news apps. Why do I do that?"

It's okay to not have the answers or explanations for why we are doing these things or feeling this way. But the goal here is to bring attention to two things. First, we reach for our devices for a variety of reasons. I often talk about how our devices are not switchblades; they are Swiss Army knives. They don't simply have one open-and-close, single-blade function. Instead, our phones are also communication tools, cameras, calendars, televisions, social media, games, news sources, weather forecasts, photo albums, and so much more. We are normalizing the variety and modeling for our children the multitool aspect of digital devices.

The second thing the exercise reminds us of is that there is an emotional component to both our reason for and the resulting experience of our tech use. Furthermore, ascribing a description to each instance of our tech use, even if we don't fully understand our reasons for doing so, helps our children realize, *Wow, screentime impacts my parent's feelings or experience in a variety of ways too. It's not just me.*

When it comes to older children and living your life out loud around screen use, I tell parents that if your tweens and teens start rolling their eyes at you every time you do it, you are probably doing it right. With practice, it gets easier. And when it comes to screentime and technology, living our lives out loud is something we can do for children at any age. It beautifully connects our use of technology to executive function skill building.

## THE BENEFITS OF LIVING OUR TECH LIVES OUT LOUD

Think about the effort required to build new habits. One of the first steps in changing the way we do something is identifying the behavior that is there in the first place. For example, if we want to eat more healthfully, we might start writing down everything we eat. The practice of logging our meals and snacks focuses our attention more on what we're choosing to eat. And if we know we are going to need to write it down, it gives us an opportunity to ask, "Am I eating this because I am hungry? Or for another reason?" And it might direct us toward making a different choice.

When we do this for screen use, we are bringing our awareness to how we use devices. For now, this refers to adult use of screens. Children can live their lives out loud too, but it starts with how *we* do it, in earshot of them and other family members.

When we live our life out loud, we're doing several really important things. We model when and how we use technology and bring attention and awareness to our screentime. In doing so, we practice accountability for our personal device use. We also show our children that our devices are multitools, and we can model an emotional vocabulary for how our devices make us feel. And we also build executive function skills by explaining out loud the steps in a process, showing how we manage our time, or modeling how our use of technology affects our emotions.

Articulating our tech use and our feelings about it requires practice. It's awkward at first. But as many of my clients tell me, the more they do it, the more they are aware of others who do *not* do it and how curious it makes them—that is, it makes them wonder, *Why aren't you telling me why you're looking at your phone?*

The scientists who study children and screentime agree with this approach of living our lives out loud; they just describe it differently. For example, in a November 2016 policy statement titled "Media and Young Minds" and published in the journal *Pediatrics*, the American Academy of Pediatrics recommended that caregivers limit screen use for children between the ages of two and five to one hour a day of "high-quality programming."[22] They also suggested that parents watch those programs with their children so that they could help

---

22  David Hill, MD; Nusheen Ameenuddin, MD; Yolanda (Linda) Reid Chassiakos, MD; Corinn Cross, MD; Jeffrey Hutchinson, MD; Alanna Levine, MD; Rhea Boyd, MD; Robert Mendelson, MD; Megan Moreno, MD; and Wendy Sue Swanson, MD, "Media and Young Minds," *Pediatrics*, Volume 138, Issue 5, November 2016, https://publications.aap.org/pediatrics/article/138/5/ e20162591/60503/Media-and-Young-Minds.

their children comprehend and apply what they were viewing to the world. In the same issue of *Pediatrics*, the academy didn't recommend a specific amount of time for school-age children and adolescents to spend on media use but instead stressed the importance of parents setting consistent limits, continuing to watch programming with their children, and having ongoing conversations about screen use. Those discussions reflect the same principles as living our tech lives out loud.

## DEFINING A NEW NORMAL

When it came to screen use during the pandemic, many of us opted— or were forced—to change how we did things. Sometimes that was wonderful: being able to stay connected to friends and family while we were in lockdown, for example. Unfortunately, it also meant increased screentime for school, work, and entertainment, and that made parenting more challenging.

We have to assume best intentions—parents did the best they could with what they had. But when the world began to return to its pre-COVID routines and behaviors, our device use didn't necessarily change back: screentime remained high and became a greater source of family conflict. Consequently, some children emerged more resilient whereas some children emerged far worse off.[23] Either way, we were facing a new normal.

Even if we want to, we can't return to prepandemic screentime rules. And we have to adjust to numerous other changes too. First, children are older than they were when the pandemic started, and many have gone through developmental shifts since then. Second, just as the pandemic shifted the way we interact with one another in person, it also impacted the way we used technology to connect,

---

23   For more on COVID's impact on children, see *The Stolen Year* by Anya Kamenetz.

socialize, learn, work, and entertain ourselves; what worked before (if it did) will not work now. Third, schools invested heavily in digital technology tools during the pandemic in the name of remote learning (though many were already spending heavily before COVID), and there is widespread public pressure from taxpayers who want to see those digital tools used. Given these here-to-stay shifts, what matters is how we move into the new normal.

Before the pandemic, there were still quite a few families who limited or restricted their children's exposure to screentime—those who might even be called screen free. But it was also easier to move about the world and find tech-free places, including at school. Today, however, it is much more difficult—if not nearly impossible—to avoid screen-based technologies. Restaurant menus, QR codes, cashless parking meters and shops, online banking, and even virtual doctor's appointments are much more the norm. It's no wonder that the authors of the book *Screen Schooled*, veteran classroom teachers who have written about the damaging effects of tech overuse and misuse, say that asking kids not to be distracted by technology is akin to holding an Alcoholics Anonymous meeting in a bar.[24]

This means that any approach to a postpandemic parenting strategy for managing screentime will have to consider that screen-based technology is ubiquitous. And again, a highly effective approach to managing all this is to bring our attention—and our children's attention—to how we use technology and devices by living our lives out loud.

## LIVING OUR LIVES OUT LOUD WILL KEEP US FROM PHUBBING

Our devices have a way of sucking us in. I stopped wearing a watch because I just used my phone to tell the time. Unfortunately, pulling

---

24   Joe Clement and Matt Miles, *Screen Schooled* (Chicago, IL: Chicago Review Press, October 2017).

my phone out to look at the clock meant I was likely to also look at my email or check a text message. And I'm sure many of us have been guilty of "just checking our phones" while talking with friends or family.

Phubbing has been around for a while—pretty much since we started putting phones in our pockets. But when Apple Watches came out in 2015, suddenly we could phub with even greater subtlety. We could look as though we were checking the time on our watch, but really, we were reading an incoming text. The effect on the friend or listener, however, is the same: we had phubbed them.

My husband once made this astute observation: "Texting is giving someone who isn't even in the room permission to interrupt you." Most adults hate the feeling of being phubbed in the middle of a conversation, but many of us don't know what to say in response. So we say nothing and keep talking or wait for their attention to return. Either way, being phubbed doesn't feel great.

Similarly, when we phub our children, who rarely understand what we're looking at on our phones in the first place, what they witness is that some anonymous ping is powerful enough to pull our attention completely away from whatever is happening in the moment, and that feels terrible and frustrating. But because children tend to be more honest, raw, and real than polite adults, they will let us know in words or actions that they don't want our phones to be more important to us than they are.

There is an easy solution to address phubbing: live our lives out loud. Now, we are putting an explanation to the behavior. We are helping our children understand, even if they don't like it, why our attention might be getting pulled in another direction. And ultimately, we get to hold ourselves to a higher standard of behavior, in which the presence of a physical person is valued more than an anonymous person who isn't even in the same room.

Even better, living our lives out loud helps our children see that we struggle too. We can teach our children that this is a skill to work on. We can show them that our devices affect our emotional state and that they are right: sometimes, our attention *is* unfairly pulled away from them. As we reach for our phones, we can ask, "How does it make me feel? Why am I reaching for this? In my moment of boredom, I'm making this choice." Then, we have an opportunity to talk about these experiences with our children and work toward more tech-intentional habits.

## WE'RE ALL PERFECT SCREENTIME PARENTS—UNTIL WE AREN'T

Many parents of younger children believe they've got a handle on screentime. They have limits. They monitor content. They co-view. They can take away the iPad or hide it. But somewhere around age 10, there is an abrupt shift. It might be the preadolescent brain changes and the early onset of puberty. It might be that it seems like all their peers are getting their first smartwatches or smartphones (indeed, over 50% of American children have a phone by age 11). It may be the normal development shift from preoperational to concrete operational thinking. It may be some combination of all these things.

Suddenly, well-intentioned, thoughtful parents who have done an excellent job so far of restricting their child's use of technology and carefully monitoring content find themselves navigating an avalanche of information, peer pressure (from fellow adults as well as that experienced by their children), and little experience or understanding of what it means to be a tween in the digital age.

How do I know? Because I was such a parent. With my own son, we set limits. We restricted content. We didn't allow devices in the bedrooms. We co-viewed shows. We allowed only a few games. We asked other parents about their screen use and rules. We were proud of our excellent parenting skills.

Then, he entered middle school. Nearly every single one of his peers had a smartphone.

We had anticipated this. We knew he'd be one of the few without, but we stayed strong. We talked about why we were holding off. We folded our decision into our values. We listened when he felt frustrated. We made sure he had other opportunities to connect with friends. We also knew he would see things on his friends' phones while riding the bus to school. We told him he could always blame us if he felt embarrassed for not having a smartphone. We explained what porn was and not to hide it if he saw something he didn't understand. We emphasized the importance of letting us know about anything he saw or witnessed online that made him uncomfortable.

We got him a flip phone so that at least he could have his own phone number and his friends could text him. But the rule was that the phone had to stay at home; after all, he was at school with his friends all day, so, we reasoned, why would he need a phone when he was with them? To text, his flip phone used the predictive texting feature, which annoyed him but also had the advantage of limiting how much time he wanted to spend on his flip phone.

Then, COVID happened. At the end of his first year of middle school, like so many children around the world, our son was suddenly isolated from all his peers, taking classes on Microsoft Teams, where no one turned on their cameras. Many adolescents understandably felt completely cut off from the outside world. At a time in their development when practicing social skills was paramount, we instead sent them to their rooms for months—and even years in some locations (in my city, public school students were kept out of full-time, in-person learning environments for 403 days, not returning to full-time instruction until the fall of 2021). Middle school, already a turbulent period in a child's life, had become even more challenging.

In many ways, we were lucky that our son was ending sixth grade when the pandemic started because it meant that we could delay, for a little longer, the pressure that came with seeing all the other kids with their devices while attending school in person. But he was also missing out on all that in-person socialization that is so important to development at that age. So we expanded our rules a little to allow him to chat or play Minecraft online with friends to keep him connected socially, but we were spared the pressure to get him a smartphone earlier, and we were able to keep some screentime limits in place because he was home so much during this time period.

My son is now in high school. He has a smartphone. He does not use social media, but he uses his phone a lot more than I would like. His school, like most high schools, doesn't have an away-for-the-day policy. We have frequent conversations about what it means to be looking down instead of up. I'm constantly reminding him to sit up straight because I see how his posture has changed from hunching over his device. But in general, we have been able to work with him to moderate his screen use: we allow him some time for video games with friends, scrolling, or playing online chess, and sometimes we ask him to put it away. Mostly, he complies.

I realized it wasn't our limit setting when he was young that has made these teen years a little easier. What had the biggest impact on our ability to stay calm when talking about devices and behavior was that for several years, my husband and I had been living our lives out loud around our own screen use. We had been owning that we struggled too. We had been trying to model the behavior we wanted to see—and to make positive changes when we messed up.

And our son would call us out on it. He'd say, "Stop looking at your phone." This was hard to hear, but he was usually right. And our reaction to this mattered a lot: we could've been defensive and scolded him for being rude to us. But if we paused and looked more closely, we were the ones being rude. We weren't practicing what we preached.

This is the hardest part of becoming tech-intentional. If we want things to be different with our children's screen use, it doesn't start with time limits or monitoring. It starts with us taking a deep breath when our kid calls us out, saying, "Thank you for pointing that out. I'm trying to do better, and I missed this one." And it means making sure they know that it's okay for them to inform us when they aren't feeling seen.

Let me add in one more thing about my own parenting experience with screens thus far. I have a second child, a daughter. She is as genetically related to my husband and me as our son is, but she couldn't be more different in nearly every way from her brother. That's okay; it's wonderful, in fact. But all the rules and limits we had for our son have been modified and adapted for our daughter. At age 11, she is already asking for a smartphone, keeps "forgetting" to ask permission to use a device, and is easily getting sucked down digital rabbit holes. She is also incredibly tech savvy: at the start of remote learning, she figured out how to hack Zoom meetings, with very little instruction, just before the platform added the password feature (thankfully, she hadn't yet been successful in Zoombombing any sessions!). It's a great example of how great the temptation is to tinker and experiment—out of purely normal childish curiosity—with any new technology. But developmentally speaking, we need to see a little more of those formal operational skills of understanding the benefits and consequences of screen use in place before we give her a personal smartphone.

Although our children are so different in personality, what hasn't changed—and what is still allowing us to parent in a tech-intentional way—is how we use devices around our daughter. We are still narrating what we do as we do it. We are owning our shortcomings. We are trying to show her that we are constantly working at it. In other words, we are living our lives out loud.

Millions of families are navigating the screentime challenges of the modern era. And even within our family, different approaches must be taken for different children. It is why a one-size-fits-all approach to screentime won't work. It's one of many reasons parental controls aren't the solution we want them to be. In lieu of one simple solution, living our lives out loud is the single most important strategy we can implement as parents in our path to becoming tech-intentional.

## FUTURE-PROOFING STARTS TODAY

I often say it is the parents of children over 10 who find me but the parents of children under 10 who need me. My challenge is to show parents of younger children what is coming and help them get ready *before* they cross over into the smartphone or social media world.

Time and time again, parents tell me that they wish they had delayed their children's access to smart devices and social media. There are so many devastating stories about children whose lives have been deeply, negatively, and sometimes permanently impacted by the use of digital technology. It is important to listen to those parents who have gone before us, who have experienced these hardships, and who share the lessons they have learned.

My former parent clients have shared some startling and eye-opening examples. One son was so addicted to his phone that he would put it in a plastic bag and take it into the shower with him. A daughter spent so much time on toxic social media sites that she lost sleep and started to self-harm. Another parent understandably complained, "A random YouTuber has more influence on my tween than I do." Still another didn't know what to do when a stranger's avatar

assaulted their child's avatar inside an online game.[25] In daily headlines, we confront cautionary tales about cyberbullying, social media
gone horribly wrong, and sextortion. It is no secret that young people
are experiencing extreme mental health challenges and increased
rates of suicide. Current research now indicates that social media
isn't just correlated with young people's mental health struggles; it is
indeed a cause of them.

As parents, we know that children are struggling, and we know
that excessive tech use can exacerbate and complicate their pain.
This is why it's so important to start our tech-intentional habits when
they're still young. Think about it this way: long before our children
turn 16, we teach them about car safety. We place them in car seats
when they're infants and toddlers. Later, we teach them to wear seat
belts. Before they earn their licenses, we enroll them in driver's ed,
give them lots of opportunities to practice safe driving, and model
good driving habits ourselves. Just like with cars, safely and respon-
sibly operating a smartphone must come with similar scaffolding,
rooted in a strong sense of family values and the knowledge that we
are in this together.

These preventative measures mean more work for us. I know it
feels like a lot. But if digital devices are going to play a role in our
lives, then how we use them—and how we talk about how we use
them—around our children matters. Living our lives out loud is one
crucial step in becoming a tech-intentional parent. It's not about
looking at our phones less; it's about looking at our phones intentionally. It's about bringing our use of technology from the background to
the foreground. It's ultimately about what we do, not just what we say.

---

25   In my work with families, I am very clear about my professional role. I am not a licensed mental
     health professional. In all these examples, the families were also working with therapists and
     doctors to help their children. As a consultant and educator, I offered these parents concrete
     strategies to implement in conjunction with the support of their medical team.

## TL;DR

- Screentime is everywhere. Even if we want to avoid it, we can't.

- Living our lives out loud is the secret sauce to becoming tech-intentional.

- Future-proofing starts today.

# CHAPTER 6

# IT'S NOT A FAIR FIGHT: PERSUASIVE DESIGN

Behavior change is not as complicated
as most people think . . . it's systematic.

—B. J. FOGG

There are only two industries that call their
customers "users": illegal drugs and software.

—EDWARD TUFTE

**"IT'S TIME TO TURN OFF THE IPAD,"** I tell my eight-year-old daughter, who is sprawled on the floor, absorbed in a game called Animal Jam.

No response.

"Sylvie, did you hear me? It's time to turn off the iPad."

Silence. Her face glows blue in the light of the screen. She taps the screen vigorously with her index finger.

"Sylvie! Your time is up. It is *time to turn off the iPad*!" She registers the sound of my voice by nodding slightly but is so absorbed in the game, I'm certain she has no idea what I said, let alone how many times I've said it.

As I'm about to turn up the volume on my mom voice, she suddenly speaks: "Oh my gosh, Mom! I got a sapphire!" She is so genuinely excited it throws me off for a second.

"What are you talking about?" I ask, exasperated. "I mean—never mind! Give me the iPad. Your time is up, and I am tired of repeating myself." I bend down to take the device. She clutches it closer, her eyes still glued to the screen.

"Mom! Nooooooo! You can't take it yet! I'm about to do a fashion show, and all these friends are waiting! I can't stop now!" she continues, furiously tapping the screen, hunched over, eyes unblinking.

"Sylvie, I don't want to fight about this—you agreed to hand it over when your time was up! If you don't give it to me in the count of five, I am going to take it!"

5 ... 4 ... 3 ... 2 ... 1 ...

Cue: MELTDOWN.

Even as The Screentime Consultant, I have struggled to transition my own children away from screens. There is cajoling, resisting, pleading, and negotiating; sometimes, yelling and relenting; and often, a sense of complete failure as a parent.

I know I am not alone in this experience. Every single parent I know has wondered about screentime: How do I get them to turn screens off without a fight? How much is too much? How do we protect our children? When do I get them a phone? What about peer pressure? What rules should I set?

Despite any well-intentioned efforts, we still often end up exhausted, mad, and defeated. But there is a reason why so many of us relent and just end up saying yes, even if we don't want to: the apps, games, platforms, and devices our children use are designed to keep their attention, and when a child's attention is hijacked like that, the meltdowns and fights are inevitable.

It's not a fair fight.

## TECH'S SECRET WEAPON

It turns out that we're not bad parents. Well, I suppose it depends on the day and which kid we ask, but for the most part, it isn't our fault that the screentime battles end the way they do. But why does it feel so much harder to peel away an iPad than a book? Why do the emotional outbursts after social media scrolling seem disproportionate to the general grumbling of being asked to do a chore?

It's because Big Tech's secret weapon is something called persuasive design, and it's the biggest technological difference between our childhood and our children's current reality. Persuasive design applies human psychology to technology. In turn, companies use the power of technology to influence and change our behavior.

A few years ago, only tech industry insiders were familiar with the term *persuasive design*. But the hard work of scientists, medical experts, and nonprofits such as Fairplay; documentaries such as *Screenagers* and *The Social Dilemma*; books such as Adam Alter's *Irresistible*, Johann Hari's *Stolen Focus*, and Max Fisher's *The Chaos Machine*; and the efforts of concerned educators, activists, and parents who knew where to look and how deep to dig have all helped increase public awareness. What these experts have revealed is that with new developments in technology changing rapidly over the past couple of decades, so also has the user experience shifted. Tech companies and app developers make money from advertising, which means they need us to spend more time engaging with their products. When platforms and apps capture our attention for longer, tech company profits increase. And developers and designers quickly realized that *how* they built their products determined how long we stayed online. To persuade us to engage longer, design features needed to tap into the dopamine in our brains.

When it comes to taking away the iPad or shutting off the video game or stopping the social media scroll, parents need to understand that this hijacking of dopamine is *why* it is so difficult to end the screentime battles. Dopamine is often thought of as the pleasure hormone, which is why things like food, sex, and drugs make us feel good. But dopamine is also involved in seeking behavior. This means that dopamine impacts our desire for something and compels us to seek out more of the thing we want. For children, tweens, and teens, then, playing on a tablet or scrolling through social media is not unlike substance use: the dopamine in their brains drives their desire to stay on longer, which means they will fight parents even harder when it is time to turn them off. As Ramsay Brown, neuroscientist and cofounder of Boundless Mind, a platform that uses AI and neuroscience to predict, shape, and analyze behavior, stated in 2018: "Your kid is not weak willed because he can't get off his phone . . . Your kid's brain is being engineered to get him to stay on his phone."[26]

In other words, it's not a fair fight.

As parents, we are fighting our child's dopamine levels, not our child. And dopamine has impacts on other areas of our health too. Our nervous system uses dopamine as a messenger to send information between cells. Too much or too little of this neurotransmitter can result in a wide range of health issues, ranging from ADHD to addiction. The peaks of dopamine levels caused by certain types of screentime—and the ways that excessive device use make those

---

26  Haley Sweetland Edwards, "You're Addicted to Your Smartphone. This Company Thinks It Can Change That," *Time*, April 13, 2018, https://time.com/5237434/youre-addicted-to-your-smartphone-this-company-thinks-it-can-change-that/.

feel-good pathways less sensitive, requiring more and more stimulation to experience that sense of pleasure—are a recipe for adolescent mental health crises. No wonder youth today are struggling.

Adults struggle too. Our use of digital technology falls neatly into this dopamine cycle. Much like gambling or drugs, our own screen use taps into those neural pathways that tell our brains and bodies, "Oooh, we like this! Do this more!" Tristan Harris, a former Google ethicist and cofounder of the Center for Humane Technology, says our phones have become so addictive that they are essentially "slot machines in our pockets."[27] When it comes to the dopamine loop, slot machines are appealing—and can be highly addictive—because we don't win all the time; we only win some of the time, and we don't win at regular intervals. This is similar to what makes our phones, tablets, and social media so desirable to our brains—we *might* get a notification, a new email, or a new like. If we as adults are just as susceptible to this dopamine release, then it's easier to understand why our children fight us so hard when it comes time to power down.

Here is a visual of how the dopamine feedback loop works when we spend time on social media:

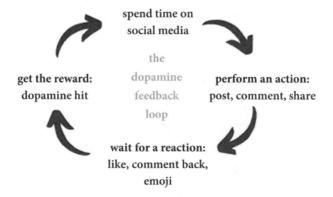

27   Tristan Harris, "The Slot Machine in Your Pocket," *Spiegel International*, July 27, 2016, https://www.spiegel.de/international/zeitgeist/smartphone-addiction-is-part-of-the-design-a-1104237.html.

Our rewards—the likes, the reactions, the comments—come at irregular intervals, making them more appealing. Behavioral psychologists call this *intermittent variable rewards*. Back in the days of the old-school Blackberry, push notifications at regular intervals (e.g., every 15 minutes) meant our devices were much less addictive than modern ones because we could predict exactly when our content would arrive. The push notifications or alerts on our smartphones today, however, arrive randomly (unless we schedule them otherwise), driving our desire to check for new messages to ridiculously compulsive levels.

Why does this matter? Brains like predictability, and when we don't get something at a predictable rate, we feel compelled to keep playing, scrolling, or checking our device because *this* time, we *might* win, get a like, or receive a new email. How many times have we closed a tab or social media app only to open it seconds later without thinking about it? Our brains want to check for a new message . . . just in case. And each time we do this, we get that pleasure response of dopamine, which makes us feel good, want more, and go right back to doing it again. Our brains love intermittent variable rewards. Each time we receive one, our nervous system sends surges of pleasure hormones through our bodies. It physically feels good when we get this digital feedback. This is why our children don't want to stop playing their games or watching videos. The unpredictability of content and feedback keeps them wanting to continue the experience, even when it causes conflict for the family.

Even more challenging is that our brains and bodies adapt to the variability. The reason our screentime battles feel more fraught every time is that each new dopamine surge isn't as intense as the previous one. Our children need to stay on longer to get that same level of feel-good hormones, which means spending more time on their devices. This results in an even bigger fight with parents when screentime is over.

If you're thinking, *Yes, I know all this. But I can put my phone down whenever I want. I'm aware but in control*, consider the following: Have you ever said to yourself, "Just one more episode" when binge-watching Netflix—and lo, several episodes later, you finally realized how late it is? Have you ever taken a break from work to scroll through social media but ended up down a rabbit hole of links? Ever used a fitness app or watch to track your steps and then felt compelled to check, compare, match, or beat your previous mileage? Have you accepted the suggestion of an algorithm to purchase a book or watch a new movie? Ever felt anxious or stressed when a notification or alert signifies a new text or email and draws you back to your device?

If any of the previous examples resonated, you have experienced persuasive design. And even with fully formed brains, not only are we very susceptible to these techniques, but we are also very likely to deny that it affects us—which is all part of the design.

It's one thing to face persuasive design elements as an adult. But persuasive design impacts children in a far more insidious way: technology companies hire developmental psychologists to help them build products that are irresistible to children. They market their products to parents. We hand them over to our children, who can't help but check just one more time, click one more link, or watch one more show. Then, we watch them fall apart when it's time to relinquish the screen because of the way the technology is intentionally designed to tap into their neural pathways and spike their dopamine.

Some authors, such as Nir Eyal, would argue that all of this is a matter of willpower and that we can simply choose to put down our devices. I disagree. Persuasive design makes it difficult for even adults to manage their screen use. For children, whose brains are still developing, it is absolutely not within their control. Parents play a role in this, but much more pressure needs to be applied to technology companies to make their features less addictive. Until that is more profitable than current business practices, however, we can only recall the pointed words of

Edward Tufte, a Yale professor emeritus of political science, statistics, and computer science: "There are only two industries that call their customers 'users': illegal drugs and software."[28]

## THE EVOLUTION OF PERSUASIVE DESIGN

How did we even get here?

The father of persuasive technology is a man named B. J. Fogg. An adjunct professor at Stanford, he is also the founder and director of the university's Behavior Design Lab, which was formerly known as the Stanford Persuasive Technology Lab. In 2007, Professor Fogg gave his students an assignment: design an app, get as many people to use it as possible, and keep them coming back. Using persuasive design, his students generated a variety of free apps for Facebook, and almost overnight they were able to draw in millions of new users—and, along with them, a lot of advertising revenue.

Now dubbed the Facebook Class, more than two dozen participants from this original group laid the path for an entrepreneurial methodology known as the lean start-up. The quick success of these students caught the attention of nearby Silicon Valley executives and investors: If college kids at Stanford could generate that many users that quickly, could Silicon Valley translate this into profit? It turns out that they could, and as a result, start-up tech culture exploded. Things then changed rapidly. Between October 2007, when Fogg first challenged his students, and August 2008, the number of Facebook users leapt from 50 million to 100 million.[29] By 2022, the social media juggernaut had nearly three billion *daily* active users.

---

28  Edward Tufte, *The Social Dilemma*, Netflix, 2020.

29  Miguel Helft, "The Class that Built Apps, and Fortunes," *New York Times*, May 7, 2011, https://www.nytimes.com/2011/05/08/technology/08class.html.

As the tech industry has expanded exponentially, many tech leaders would have us believe that there is nothing *really* nefarious about our ubiquitous devices and apps. Programmers and developers who implement persuasive design also speak of its positive potential, suggesting that digital apps can help people get rid of bad behaviors, such as forgetting to floss, or encourage good ones, such as weight loss. These designers tap into our emotions, such as stimulating feel-good dopamine pathways, to create and shape our habits. However, while all emotions are valid, not all *behaviors* resulting from emotions are reasonable. For instance, we might feel really angry at someone, but that indignation or rage might grow into a refusal to communicate, take someone else's perspective, or resolve the conflict (one of my favorite quotes is "Resentment is like taking poison and waiting for the other person to die"). Other emotions, like shame, might lead us to self-medicate or self-harm.

Additionally, persuasive design—even that purported to help us develop positive habits—is problematic because it is manipulative. Some might argue that being manipulated to floss our teeth more regularly or lose weight is a good thing because it's beneficial to our oral and physical health. But if we're okay with that form of behavior change, then we might become more susceptible to the kinds of manipulation that lead to self-destructive habits, such as excessive screentime.

And when it comes to our children, allowing devices to influence or control them in an unscrupulous way should not be part of a healthy parenting approach. The tech companies whose target market is children, tweens, and teens hire behavioral psychologists and other experts in child development who study the impact emotions play in their decision-making. This becomes deeply problematic when we consider the very real and destructive reality of the products they help design. These researchers and engineers of persuasive design know that we humans are motivated by the way we feel, by how we are perceived by others, and by our need for acceptance and approval. However, the dark side of technology is that it manipulates *all* our emotions to change our behavior. For adults, this is hard enough. For children, who have not-yet-fully-developed brains, this is cruel.

The technology industry doesn't want parents to think that our children are being influenced or conditioned because that might make us less likely to allow our kids to interact with their product, which means lower profit margins. Sometimes, technology companies will even try to put a positive spin on persuasive design's effects on young users so that they don't look like the bad guys: flashy, attractive graphics that look like child-friendly cartoons catch our eye; industry-funded research soothes our concerns; schools promote "educational" tools to help overworked teachers. By packaging and pitching to us in such a way that these features seem harmless, tech companies persuade parents to feel less guilty when we give in to more game time or let our six-year-old download TikTok. Yet manipulating *anyone's* behavior, especially children's, even in the name of building good habits or skills, is, well, *not* good.

The technology industry's use of persuasive technologies is unethical and immoral, particularly as it manipulates children. The work we do now as parents is so important; becoming tech-intentional means fighting for our children's future cognitive and emotional well-being and interrupting the coercive, habit-forming techniques that interfere with healthy brain development. We would never dream of testing the addictiveness of cigarettes on young children, yet we are letting technology companies test the addictiveness of their products on our children's brains. Big Tech today is yesterday's Big Tobacco.

Some litigation of harms done by social media companies and congressional testimony by former and current Big Tech executives are pushing lawmakers to act. But new technology moves at a rapid pace, legislation at a glacial one—and in the meantime, it is our children who are the guinea pigs. So what are parents to do? At this point, we are frequent users of big platforms ourselves, and the idea of going without feels like an impossibility. Our email accounts, our documents, our photographs, our text messages, our internet searches are all connected to one or more of the big technology platforms, and we know, at least on some level, that our digital moves are being tracked, measured, and evaluated (e.g., when we notice our internet searches appear in our social media feeds or learn that Google is both the most visited website in the world and, raking in over $100 billion in annual sales in 2018, a highly profitable advertising company). We want so desperately to protect our children's fragile neural pathways from exploitation, but we are up against a heavily funded industry that wants to capture and keep our attention as long as possible. It's no wonder we feel like David to technology's Goliath. As I tell parents regularly, while it is not our *fault* that persuasive design exists, it remains our *job* as parents to teach our children about it and work to protect them—and ourselves—from the long arm of the tech industry. Next to climate change, this is the fight of our parenting generation.

Some of you might be thinking, *Well, now that I know about persuasive design, I can avoid letting it manipulate me.* Unfortunately, not only are adults also susceptible to manipulative design techniques, but when we are glued to our devices, we are more likely to react harshly to our children when they interrupt us.

## USING POSITIVE DISCIPLINE TO COMBAT PERSUASIVE DESIGN

The pandemic raised new screentime challenges on top of the anxiety, fear, remote-learning issues, and social isolation of living during a pandemic. Even before COVID-19, parents told me, "My kid flies into a rage when he has to turn off the Xbox," "My tween is so moody and refuses to engage with me," and "All my kid wants to do is play on the tablet, and when I take it away, she says she has nothing else to do."

What frustrates and stymies parents the most are the emotional meltdowns: the tears, the anger, the nasty words, and even the physicality, like hitting or kicking when the device is removed. We don't know how to respond or what to do, so we give in or give up. The fight feels too fraught. But we need to understand that children—and teenagers are indeed still children—have meltdowns when screentime is up because they are experiencing a biological, persuasive-design-induced withdrawal.

These meltdowns are not because our children are bad or weak. From a child's perspective, when we take away a device, we are interrupting the flow of feel-good hormones, such as dopamine, surging through their bodies. We are taking away the very thing making them feel so wonderful. It's no surprise they completely fall apart; who wants to stop feeling amazing?

Transitions are always hard with kids, and today, of course, persuasive design makes parenting even more challenging, so how we respond matters. Recall from chapter 3 our discussion of the Parenting Quadrant. Say we are dealing with a child whose neural pathways have been hijacked by persuasive design, a tween who wants a smartphone because everyone else does, or a teen who says they're the only one without social media. What follows are some examples of how a parenting response might look for each approach.

The permissive parent says, "I want my child to fit in. If they don't have a phone or social media, she will be left out. My choice to give a phone, social media access, or excessive screentime is about my own insecurities or anxieties as an adult. It's hard for me to say no. I want my child to like me and to be my friend."

The authoritarian parent says, "You don't get everything you want.

I don't care if your friends all have it. You live in my house, under my rules, and you will do as I say, not necessarily as I do, because I am the adult and I know better. If you break the rules, you will be punished."

The neglectful parent says, "Do whatever you want on your phone. I honestly couldn't care less. I use social media all the time. It's what everyone does these days. Figure it out yourself. Don't come to me with your problems. It's not my job."

The positive discipline parent says, "It feels important to you to be connected to your friends. I can understand that. I also have concerns about keeping you safe. I think it's important for us to have some limits about what we do with screen use, but I want your input and ideas. This is hard for adults too. We need to keep the lines of communication open. This isn't going to be easy, but our relationship is important."

Do you hear yourself in one of the preceding responses? Which voice do you wish you had heard as a child? Which voice does your child hear?

Be curious, and don't judge yourself too harshly. You're doing what you know, and old habits are deeply embedded. The goal of a tech-intentional parent is the last example: a positive discipline approach. When we approach our dysregulated child with compassion and connection, set clear expectations and boundaries, and help them process feelings in a nonjudgmental way, we are setting our children and ourselves up for success in managing future screentime challenges. They learn that we are working *with* them, not against them, to find a path forward. They understand that we have concerns but also want to support their need to be connected to friends. They feel heard, not criticized, in desiring access to screentime.

In a tech-intentional family, relationships are valued, prioritized, and nurtured. Problems are faced together. Judgment is reserved.

## WHAT CAN PARENTS DO
## ABOUT PERSUASIVE DESIGN?

At the end of the day, persuasive design leads to increased time on screens, which displaces what decades of research tell us that children actually need: tactile play, boredom, and opportunities to develop interpersonal and problem-solving skills. Activities like being outside, playing, socializing with friends, and reading are the components of childhood that matter for optimal development. Excessive use of technology, coupled with the power of persuasive design, interferes with those experiences.

Children look to us for cues about how to behave; we must start by being honest and sharing accurate information with them. We can explain even to a young child how persuasive technologies hook our brains and make it so we don't want to stop watching our show or playing a game. We can teach them to identify the deep feelings that these experiences bring up and give them the vocabulary to talk about how screens affect us.

We don't give children enough credit. In our desire to protect them from difficult experiences, we sometimes soften the language or avoid the tough stuff. But when we talk to children about persuasive design, they know what we're talking about, and they get upset when they discover they are being manipulated. After all, no one likes to be tricked. But they cannot know they are being manipulated until we talk to them about it and teach them to recognize persuasive design techniques in the apps and programs they use.

As Tristan Harris of the Center for Humane Tech shared at a U.S. Senate hearing in June 2019, "One thing I have learned is that if you tell people, 'This is bad for you,' they won't listen . . . if you tell people, 'This is how you're being manipulated,' no one wants to feel manipulated." This is especially true of children, who are action-oriented, compassionate humans. In the surveys I do of schools, one of the most common responses I hear from students about the negatives of screen use is the addictive nature of devices and apps, and these critiques are coming from the very teens who use their devices multiple hours a day. Children *know* their screens present a problem, even if it doesn't appear that way.

So one of the most important things we can do as tech-intentional parents is to teach our children about the manipulative elements that drive them to want to stay on screens longer. Just as we show them how to look both ways when they cross a street or put on a helmet when riding a bike, we can teach our kids about keeping themselves—and their brains—safe when using their devices.

Because my kids have The Screentime Consultant as their mother, we talk a lot about screens and persuasive design to cement the term in their consciousness so that they will recognize it when they encounter it. For all children, an understanding of persuasive design builds over a series of conversations. Like many things in life, true learning comes from practice over time. We must have these conversations with our children early and often so that they can build their awareness, critical thinking, and media literacy skills, especially as they come of age in a digital world.

---

### PERSUASIVE DESIGN'S IMPACTS AT DIFFERENT AGES AND STAGES

**How persuasive design impacts littles**

When screentime is over, littles might respond with the following:

- A complete meltdown or tantrum that feels disproportionate to the transition
- Screaming, yelling, hitting, or throwing objects

*continued*

- An excess of energy or emotion
- Fear that if they don't keep playing, their character will die or they will lose points
- Asking parents to pay for new levels, skins (i.e., outfits), tokens, etc., to stay competitive

**How persuasive design impacts middles**

When screentime is over, middles might respond with the following:

- A constant need to check social media accounts or text conversations for fear of missing out on something, often at the expense of other activities
- Displacing sleep to stay online or on screens at night, again out of fear of missing out
- Feeling like others are relying on them to be available online (e.g., Snap Streaks)
- Carrying a heavy emotional burden to keep tabs on friends at the expense of their own health and well-being
- Frustration, anger, or aggression toward adults for setting limits or removing devices

## PRACTICAL STRATEGIES TO NAVIGATE MELTDOWNS

The post-screentime meltdown is one of the hardest parts of parenting in the digital age, which is why so many parents give in. We dread the fight and meltdown, but creating a plan ahead of time can help us respond more effectively. The following strategies can help mitigate the misery.

### Strategies and prompts for littles

- Acknowledge the difficulty your child has about stopping:
  - "I can see it is hard for you to turn off."

- "I know it's frustrating to stop doing something you enjoy."

- Settle on a specific time limit before you hand over the device:
  - "The timer will tell us it is time to turn off the iPad. I know it might be hard for you to make that transition, but I am here to help."
  - "Can we agree that 45 minutes is long enough for today? That's two episodes of your favorite show, and then we will turn it off."

- Predetermine a strategy to deal with the energy that comes with giving up the device:
  - "Before we start screentime, let's make a plan for how we can help you channel your big feelings after it's over. Would you like to run up and down the stairs?"
  - "I know when screentime is over, you will have lots of energy. How about we make a plan to go ride bikes or run around the block?"

- Acknowledge that you and your child know that a meltdown is still likely, even with all these parameters in place:
  - "That timer is our cue to wind down. Is there one last thing you want to do?"
  - "I know this is hard. Tell me about what you will do next time in this game."
  - "Time's up. What's something fun we could do now?"

- Celebrate the successes, even the really small wins:
  - "Hey! I notice that it took you only five minutes to calm down after the screentime ended, and last time it took 10 minutes!"

- "Thank you for working hard to burn off that extra energy after screentime was up. I know that is a hard transition, and I could see you making that effort!"

### Dialogue prompts for middles

- "I know this is really hard for you. How can I help you stick to the limits we establish?"

- "What do you think is a realistic amount of time to be on your phone?"

- "How do you feel when you've spent several hours gaming without a break? Would it help if I gave you a reminder to take a break?"

- "Your brain is really powerful and really wants to keep you playing, but we made an agreement, and now it's time to stop."

- "I know you're worried about missing out on important things. How can I support you in feeling connected while also making sure you're getting the brain breaks you need?"

- "I find it hard to put my phone down too. Is there something we could do together to hold each other accountable? I'm open to trying something new."

## CELEBRATE THE SUCCESSES, NO MATTER HOW SMALL

Even if a meltdown lasts five minutes less than the last, it is worth celebrating. Acknowledging positive behavior is even more important than naming the negative, because drawing attention to the positive behavior actually reinforces it. Where attention goes, energy flows.

So focus on the successes, and remember to replace judgment with curiosity, always striving to make neutral, observational statements.

We talk a lot about persuasive design in our home. That's intentional. Though their interests may change—new games, new friends, new apps—the conversations stay constant. Not long ago, Sylvie was playing Animal Jam with her friend. I overheard her friend say she didn't like another game because "all these ads pop up" and "they constantly try to get you to buy stuff."

Sylvie sighed loudly, shrugged her shoulders, and said, "Yeah. That's called 'persuasive design,' and my mom talks about it *all* the time."

## TL;DR

- Children's brains are not adult brains; they are far less developed than ours.

- Persuasive design grabs hold of—and profits from—our children's attention; it is the reason it's hard for kids to stop using screens. It's not a fair fight.

- Our parenting style impacts how we respond to our child's demand for screentime; we must therefore be a tech-intentional parent.

- We are supporting and enhancing our kids' well-being by setting limits and saying no to excessive screentime.

# CHAPTER 7

# CONNECTION AS THE ANTIDOTE TO EXCESSIVE SCREEN USE

*The opposite of addiction isn't sobriety; it is connection.*

—JOHANN HARI, AUTHOR[30]

**AVOCADOS ARE DELICIOUS.** But they're also tricky. If we buy them when they're firm, we have to wait a few days until they're ripe enough to eat. But if we wait too long, they're brown and mushy.

There's a popular meme that shows the stages of an avocado ripening over the course of a week. Below the unripe avocado are the words "not yet." The next day, the same thing: "not yet." On the third day, we get another "not yet." And on days four and five, it's still "not yet."

Then, on the sixth day, "too late."

What do avocados have to do with parenting in the digital age? At least in relation to an avocado's ripening process, quite a bit.

---

30  Johann Hari, *Chasing the Scream* (London: Bloomsbury, 2016).

When children reach age 10, several big things happen. First, brains are undergoing dramatic changes. Social rewards become much more important, so kids want to spend more time with their friends. Spending time with friends means paying more attention to fitting in and social approval. This age group tries on new identities and styles as they figure out their role in the social hierarchy. These are the preteen years of early adolescence, when the scales tip from desiring parental approval to seeking peer approval. (This is normal, by the way, and has been happening for decades.)

But for today's 10-year-olds, there is a very big environmental difference. As tweens are entering this new stage of brain development, they are simultaneously given increased access to smartphones, gaming, and social media on top of increased screen use for schoolwork. By the time they turn 11, over half of American children have their own smartphone.

One of the reasons I hear the most concerns from parents with children in this age group is that for so many years, screentime had felt relatively manageable. Suddenly, this significant brain change, accompanied by puberty and access to smartphones and social media, means that the unripe avocado we've so carefully nurtured has passed into the overripe stage, and we're left trying to handle it carefully and wondering, *Did we wait too long?*

I'm being slightly facetious. It is never too late to make meaningful changes. And overripe avocados can make delicious guacamole. Our children, however, are much more complex than fruit. And it gets much, much harder after age 10 to parent in a tech-intentional way—though it is not impossible!

As this age group increases their time online, with or without parental permission, they also bump up against the fact that online interactions are permanent and public. Their brains, while changing dramatically, will still not fully develop for another 10 or 20 years. So the ability to see that far ahead, understand consequences, and mitigate risks is not a skill they have developed yet. Having access to social media and smartphones may be fun, convenient, and popular, but from a developmental standpoint, they lack a lot of cognitive safeguards.

Finally, the 10th year of life is typically the last year of elementary school and the start of middle school, when students move into buildings with older students for the first time, learn subjects separately from different teachers, and take more responsibility for their learning and achievement. High expectations of our children need to be in line with their development. For many of us, our middle school memories—with minimal screens and no social media—were emotionally turbulent, and even traumatic, years in our life.

Those of us who felt like confident, screen-savvy parents of younger children now have a child entering middle school, hitting a new developmental stage, and asking for a phone. Suddenly, this perfect storm of circumstances and development lands with a rather devastating thud in our living rooms.

We think, *Not yet. Not yet. Not yet.* And then comes the hard-hitting realization: *Uh-oh. Too late.*

## FACING THE STORM

Those who will best weather this storm focus on connection. And no, not a fast Wi-Fi connection, but in-real-life, face-to-face, familial connection.

At some point along the path of parenting, our children become more independent. This is normal, but it can be painful and bittersweet for us. These mixed feelings make parenting tweens and teens complicated. Parents have to grieve the loss of their little children while embracing their tweens' maturation into young adulthood.

Growing children, and tweens and teens in particular, need three things: autonomy, independence, and connection. I use a slightly graphic analogy to describe what it is like to parent a teen or a precocious tween. Full of this desire for independence and growing confidence, these children roll their eyes or hold up their middle finger, whether literally or figuratively. But the connection part is there too: as they flip us off, they are also reaching out to us with their other arm for a hug, a touch, reassurance, or comfort: "F*** you, *and* I need you." Such conflicting gestures make parenting this age group challenging. It's hard not to take these moments personally. It makes our job as parents painful, humbling . . . and more important than ever.

Autonomy and independence unfold along with development, and sometimes that entails our children choosing to spend time with peers instead of with us or wanting to do something without parental help. That's okay; it's normal. But it can poke the wound a bit because for parents, this growing independence may feel like rejection. It isn't, or at least not in the adult way we think of it. We *want* our children to push away and do their own thing—they are practicing for adulthood in a safe environment, and we want to give them opportunities to try and fail when the stakes are lower. Protecting them doesn't mean sheltering them from difficult situations.

For parents, however, that means we must keep focused on connection. We have to be someone they can talk to, a nonjudgmental caregiver who can comfort them through mess-ups, a parent who can love them through their worst moments. As they venture out into the world and experience challenge and adversity, we avail ourselves to them in a way that encourages them to process and grow—without shaming or judging them.

Technology can complicate all of this. When I work with private clients, I hear stories of addiction and disconnection. One parent shares, "My child goes into complete withdrawal if I take away his phone." Another expresses frustration and sadness: "They are so distracted, they no longer communicate with me." Still another observes, "Their devices are like life support: They can't live without them." Ideally, we want to avoid getting to a point where our screen-obsessed teens take their phones into the shower in a plastic bag or stay up all night to text with a self-harming friend they don't want to abandon. For one family I worked with, the mom was so fixated on monitoring her daughter's social media pages, she stayed up until 2:00 or 3:00 a.m. to "keep her safe." But this isn't sustainable. The irony of digital connection is the disconnection it breeds in the real world and the damage real relationships sustain.

All my clients' families are well meaning. They care about their children. They think they are doing things right. But inevitably comes the avocado-like scenario of *not yet, not yet, not yet, too late*. As writer Johann Hari says, the "opposite of addiction isn't sobriety; it is connection."

Connection is the antidote to screen overuse and addiction. In fact, connection doesn't just repair excessive tech use, it's preventative. Bonding with our children, as messy as it can be sometimes, matters more than the specific rules we have about screentime. We are more likely to honor, enforce, and adjust rules when we have a healthy relationship with our family members.

But there is a bit of a conundrum here. What if we're a parent in the "not yet" group? How can we learn to see how connection in the early years, maybe even before our children touch a tablet, impacts those screen-addled tween and teen years? It is critical to spend these younger years building strong relationships so that when those middle years hit, we're strong enough to handle the onslaught of adolescence.

Becoming tech-intentional means replacing judgment with curiosity. When we understand what problematic screen use looks like in the first place, we can see when *occasional* becomes *too much*.

## WHAT IS PROBLEMATIC SCREEN USE?

Our primary concern as parents is problematic screen use, or *excessive* screentime. When it comes to the question "How much is too much screentime?" I always say, "A little is okay, and a lot is too much." Unfortunately, there isn't a single number that parents can rely on to feel satisfied that they haven't crossed some invisible line. It's not that simple. So how do we know when our children's occasional screen use has become problematic?

The pandemic changed the way we use screens, but even before the pandemic, researchers had developed a tool to measure called the Problematic Media Use Measure (PMUM). One of the big challenges researchers face when assessing device use is that not all screentime is created equal: FaceTiming with Grandma is really different from watching YouTube videos. Additionally, PMUM lead researcher and developer Sarah Domoff recognized that problematic screen use is more than just the number of hours spent using a device. The bigger issue is whether tech use is impacting other areas of our lives.

---

### SYMPTOMS OF PROBLEMATIC SCREEN USE

The following list is used in the PMUM and reported or observed by parents as warning signs of problematic screen use:

1. **Unsuccessful control:** Is it difficult for my child to stop using screens?
2. **Loss of interest:** Are devices the only things that seem to motivate my child?
3. **Preoccupation:** Are screens all my child seems to think about?
4. **Psychological consequences:** Does my child's media use interfere with family activities? Do they refuse to participate so they can be on their phones, tablets, or laptops?
5. **Serious problems:** Does my child's use of technology cause problems for the family?

---

6. **Withdrawal:** Does my child become frustrated when they cannot use screens?
7. **Tolerance:** Does the amount of time my child wants to use media keep increasing?
8. **Deception:** Does my child sneak in screentime?
9. **Using screens to escape or relieve mood:** When my child has a bad day, does screentime seem to be the only thing that helps them feel better?

Becoming a tech-intentional parent means having a preventative strategy to keep these warning signs from becoming serious problems. Let's explore the tech-intentional strategies and corresponding actions we can take to address the symptoms of excessive screen use.

## Warning Sign #1: Unsuccessful Control

Tech-intentional strategy: Teach boundaries early.
Action: Use neutral, observational statements.

Parents know the battle that comes with ending screentime. As our children get older, they react in different ways. Prevention must begin in the first days of screentime—and even before parents see it as a problem. This includes watching how we, their parents, start and stop our own screentime. Early intervention and role modeling are so important. How we use our screens is how our children will learn to use screens.

We can teach boundaries around screen use at an early age by offering neutral, observational statements about what we are seeing and experiencing when it comes to screentime. Phrases like "I notice" and "I observe" can be helpful prompts. As much as possible, simply observe without offering any commentary and without asking questions.

**For littles, this might sound like the following:**

- "I noticed you were really upset earlier when screentime ended."

- "I observed how your facial expressions changed when it was time to stop."

- "I see you love watching that show. I know it can be hard to turn it off."

**For middles, this might sound like the following:**

- "I see how angry you are about being asked to put your phone down."

- "I notice you saying this feels unfair."

- "I can see your phone is really important to you."

In making these observations, we're just naming what we see and reflecting it to our children, not offering solutions yet. Being a tech-intentional parent includes curiosity without judgment, which can be incredibly difficult at times, but neutral commentary brings awareness to our children's use of screens and helps them connect their behavior and reactions to screen use. Even more powerful is when we practice this as adults too. It's another variation on living our lives out loud.

Pay attention to the words you choose when it comes to screen use; staying neutral means avoiding any judgmental opinions of what you're observing. Avoiding a charged emotional response while simply observing what's happening leads to calmer conversations about boundaries and limits. When we avoid judging and approach with curiosity, our children will learn the lesson we are trying to teach.

## Warning Sign #2: Loss of Interest

Tech-intentional strategy: Put family values first.
Action: Identify your family's priorities.

Douglas Gentile's theory of displacement reveals that time spent on screens is time *not* spent on other activities. This is a growing challenge, especially as screen use is more accessible, connected to socializing, and often required for school. Children have lost interest in activities they used to do all the time and seem to gravitate only toward screen-based play. So if we want to avoid having phone-addicted teens, we must work backward to go forward, meaning we need to ensure that our children are engaging in activities outside of screens at a very early age. Then, we find ways to support and maintain those interests.[31]

If you can't think of anything else that will incentivize or motivate your child other than screentime, then we have a different problem. Imagine you have a big jar in front of you, with three piles: big rocks, smaller pebbles, and sand. The big rocks represent the important things in your life that deserve the bulk of your time and attention. The smaller pebbles are the smaller things. The sand is everything else. Your challenge is to fill the jar with as many rocks, pebbles, and sand as possible. Which do you start with?

If you start to fill the jar with sand, the pebbles and big rocks will have to sit on the top, and you won't have room for the big rocks. If you start with pebbles, the sand will fill the space around the pebbles, but again, there won't be much room for the big rocks. But if you

---

31 There are obvious hurdles to this. For many families, the privilege of living in safe neighborhoods and having resources to provide music lessons, extracurricular activities, and babysitters means some populations of children have more opportunities to expand their interests off screen than others. There is no question that these inequities are problematic and systemic, and while I wish I could solve them here, that's beyond the scope of this book. Please visit my website (www.thescreentimeconsultant.com) for more resources on this subject.

start with the big rocks, then add in the pebbles, and finally pour in the sand around everything, you will be able to fit them all in the jar.

When it comes to our children's interests, what are their big rocks? If their big rocks are only screen based, we're missing something. We've placed too much emphasis on the screens as something we value in our family. We've filled in our other experiences around the big rocks, which means less time for connection with one another and fewer off-screen experiences.

Just as Gentile's work on the displacement effect showed, we must start with the big rocks, and the big rocks can't be screen based. Family, sports, music, friends, art, school, sleep, religious groups—these are the big rocks. In other words, the big rocks are the experiences that fit into our family's values. If we want our children to be inspired or motivated by something other than screentime as they get older, we must start by identifying and prioritizing the big rocks in their life when they are younger.

**For littles, this might look like the following:**

- Not using screentime to incentivize behaviors that align with our family values

- Teaching our children about what we value and regularly highlighting examples of it

- Making an effort as parents of young children to use screentime as something we do only sometimes or on special occasions, not as an expectation or habit

**For middles, this might look like the following:**

- Helping them prioritize their time by supporting their interests and hobbies and finding ways for them to participate

- Continuing to teach how your values connect to the ways *you* spend time and modeling that as adults

- Using screentime as a family to connect, in line with a big rock (family) and not as isolated, private screentime (sand)

Identifying your family's big rocks is something you can do together. Parents must be role models for this. Our media use around our children ultimately predicts how they will behave on screens later.

## Warning Sign #3: Preoccupation

Tech-intentional strategy: Model behavior.
Action: Engage in nonscreen activities.

Many of us are guilty of scrolling through our phones when our kids are around. I do it too. But the scope of the screentime problem means we have to start paying attention to our own use of devices when our children are young, even before we give them direct access.

Our children are watching and learning about adulthood by observing us. This can offer us great opportunities for humility, like when our toddler curses like a sailor because they heard us using expletives or when our tween's sassiness is eerily reminiscent of the tone we take with our sister on the phone. Parents are human too. Rather than drive our imperfections underground, however, we can see them as opportunities to show our children a few things. For one, we can demonstrate that screens can be hard to put down, even for grown-ups. We can own that even grown-ups make mistakes and no one feels better after being shamed for it. We can also model for our children that when we learn from our mistakes, we grow.

Earlier, we discussed the importance of parents role modeling how we use screens. When it comes to being preoccupied with our smartphones, parents may gulp a bit. But we've already established that when we know better, we do better. This is a chance to revisit and revise our own habits. As adults, we must show our children what it looks like to be engaged in other nonscreen interests. What interests are important to the adults in our house? Do our children see us reading books? Do they observe us doing something creative or artistic? Do they watch us going out for a run or a bike ride?

Remember that where attention goes, energy flows: when we put time and attention into a variety of activities, we show our children that our interests are many. Even if our devices occupy us more than we would like, we still make efforts to engage in activities that bring us joy, calm, or fun too.

**For littles, this might look like the following:**

- Sharing your interests with your child and inviting them to join you

- Living your life out loud around your nonscreen interests to draw their attention to your varied interests

- Naming your own frustrations with how your device takes you away from the other interests you have

**For middles, this might look like the following:**

- Picking up an old (or new) hobby, such as painting or playing an instrument, and doing it intentionally when your children are around

- Inviting them to try something new with you, such as a game, a sport, or a baking project

- Looking for sources of inspiration, perhaps from a screen-based activity, that could inspire off-screen interests

This is humbling work. We can dust off some of our old hobbies and show our children that it's never too late to teach old dogs new tricks.

## Warning Sign #4: Psychological Consequences

**Tech-intentional strategy: Identify your nonnegotiables early. Action: Commit to a regular screen-free family meal.**

Unfortunately, as screen use has increased, the amount of time children spend alone with their parents has shrunk. One piece of the solution is identifying our nonnegotiables: the things we won't bend on when it comes to how screen-based technology is used in our households. Other rules can change and adjust as needed, but we've identified the ones that will remain constant. These will vary from family to family, but identifying and focusing on these nonnegotiables now, when our children are young, will make things easier later. One nonnegotiable might be spending meaningful time with our children. Parent–child bonding builds their confidence, reminds them of our support, and encourages them to take safe risks in a world that can feel so scary to all of us. It isn't about the toys we buy or the vacations we take. Connection is built into our small moments of caring, such as bedtime routines and mealtime.

Even a shared screen-based family activity, like a family movie night or video game night, can be one form of connecting. A good rule for this situation is the one-family-equals-one-screen rule for movie or game nights, meaning that the entire family gathers around a single screen and no one is using personal devices during the movie or game. But another simple, effective way to build connection is to eat a meal or two a week with your family uninterrupted by devices or distractions. Engaging in conversation, learning about each other's days, sharing a laugh, or expressing curiosity about each family member's latest interests or goals can really help us stay in tune with our children—and encourage them to see that connection is valuable outside of social media and texting.

**With littles, this might look like the following:**

- Identifying two specific meals per week that will always involve the whole family, without devices

- Including young children in making these events special and protected, such as having them help cook, pick out the menu, or select the take-out restaurant

- Making place mats or name cards

- Writing down some questions to use as discussion prompts

- Picking music to listen to in the background

**With middles, this might look like the following:**

- Acknowledging how much they would like to hang out with their friends, but be clear about which evening is the family meal.

- Inviting them to bring a riddle, a moral dilemma, a news story, or even a meme to the table to discuss and share ideas.

- Encouraging them to invite a friend to the meal if your teen will be more likely to participate. Be a role model for the friend too!

## Warning Sign #5: Serious Problems

Tech-intentional strategy: Teach the importance of consent.
Action: Have the birds, bees, and screens talk.

Sometimes screen use causes more serious problems for families. These might include legal and safety issues, such as sexting (sharing nude or sexually explicit messages), cyberbullying (using digital technology to bully), predatory grooming (gaining a child's trust with the intention of sexually abusing them), swatting (harassing an innocent person by calling in emergency responders against them), or doxxing (publishing private information about someone on the internet for malicious purposes). Many of the more serious challenges that children face in online interactions come down to issues of consent—they might not fully understand what it means for themselves or for others, and others can easily take advantage of a child who lacks that understanding.

One colleague I worked with used to tell parents that you should give a child a smartphone when you were ready for them to see porn. Pornography is everywhere and is a real hazard of online interactions. Children aren't necessarily seeking it out, but a Google search can go wrong very quickly. Similarly, any app with chat abilities provides opportunities for inappropriate contact with children. Even worse, trying to limit or block these sites can feel like digital Whac-a-Mole: once you identify and restrict access to a problematic platform, another pops up.

Because staying on top of blocking and limiting inappropriate apps is impossible, it is imperative that parents teach their children about consent, safe touching, and healthy sexuality. Even parents of very young children can start to teach these lessons early and often. Many parents dread the birds and bees talk because it is awkward and embarrassing. However, we must not only have that talk early, but we must also connect it—always—to how we interact with screens and the internet. They are inextricably linked.

**For littles, this might look like the following:**

- Teaching young children to never give out personal information on the internet (e.g., name, school, location, address, or age), no matter how friendly a stranger might seem

- Asking children of any age (yes, babies too) permission to take their photo and to post it online

- Letting children know that there are inappropriate things on the internet and that their job when, not if, they see it is to tell a trusted adult right away

- Remaining calm when children report seeing scary or inappropriate stuff, thanking them for telling us, and making sure the screen is off while we figure out what to do next

- Teaching children the correct names for anatomy so that they can give accurate information to doctors or law enforcement in the event of grooming or assault

**For middles, this might look like the following:**

- Letting them know that increased independence comes with increased responsibility

- Explaining that sometimes they won't know how to deal with certain things on the internet and that you are always available to answer questions and help them

- Teaching them why it is never okay to chat with strangers on the internet and how people sometimes pretend to be someone they're not

- Telling them to never take, post, or share nude or provocative photos of themselves or others, even with permission. In some states, these actions are felonies.

Any time a child's use of screens becomes a serious problem for the family, outside support is needed. If you aren't sure, start with your pediatrician or family doctor.

## Warning Sign #6: Withdrawal

**Tech-intentional strategy: Remind children that screen use is a privilege, not a guarantee.**
**Action: Stay firm; say no.**

Along with making sure our children are engaging in a wide variety of activities, we also need to make sure that they can stay with these off-screen activities for extended periods of time. This ability will vary depending on the age of the child, but we must give them opportunities to flex and grow this muscle.

If our children get regularly frustrated when they cannot use screens, we're tipping into one of the warning signs of problematic use. If a child withdraws from activities they previously enjoyed, we've got a problem. These products, apps, and games are designed to hook and hold our attention, and when we deny our child's access to that dopamine hit, it feels like withdrawal.

One family I worked with found that their six-year-old no longer wanted to go to the playground because she wanted iPad time instead. It became so problematic that eventually she refused to eat dinner without the tablet beside her.

The antidote to withdrawal, not surprisingly, is teaching children from an early age that screentime is a privilege, not a right or a guarantee. When children are young, it's easy to fall into the after-school habits of watching some shows or playing on an iPad. But the problem this sets up for the future is that it becomes a regular expectation: "When I get home from school, I get screentime." And when it doesn't happen, a child feels entitled and bereaved and wants to know, "When do I get that screentime back?"

Some parents find success in setting specific daily limits. Another option is to vary the time, duration, and frequency of screentime to keep it unpredictable in a good way. It's like going to the ice cream shop for a treat on occasion: children don't learn to expect the experience daily, but they do get to enjoy it occasionally.

Families of young children can start thinking about this now: Does setting up a predictable routine make the demand for it higher or lower? It's okay that some children need a predictable routine; parents can still vary it by allowing regular access every two or three days—as long as they're not making it a daily expectation, for example. Additionally, consider how your child responds if they don't get their expected screentime: Are they able to occupy themselves with another activity? How your family answers these questions affects which strategy works best.

Parents have the right to say no when it comes to setting limits that safeguard our children. Just keep in mind that it is much harder to say no when kids already have a phone or social media account than it is to say no to one more episode of their favorite show or 10 more minutes of their app-based game when they are younger.

**For littles, this might look like the following:**

- Varying the time, duration, and frequency of screentime so it doesn't become too predictable

- Saying yes sometimes and saying no sometimes

- Reminding children that screen use is a privilege, not a guarantee—it's something that is special, not expected

**For middles, this might look like the following:**

- Reminding tweens and teens that having a personal device is a responsibility, not a right—and clarifying what their responsibilities are

- Teaching them when and where they can look at their phone or should put it away (e.g., at school, at a wedding, with friends, or at the dinner table)

- Letting them be mad at you—it's normal for kids not to like it when we say no; say it anyway

## Warning Sign #7: Tolerance

**Tech-intentional strategy: Combat persuasive design.**
**Action: Rank your tech options; choose the best alternative.**

The way that the dopamine loop contributes to our increased use of screens is a huge part of this problem. Tolerance entails our child wanting to spend an increasing amount of time on their devices. Each time they indulge in screentime, they must play or watch longer to get that same level of dopamine as last time, which therefore increases the amount of time they're spending on the screen.

Children are not small adults. Their brains lack the ability to regulate this behavior or even identify it as a problem. The antidote to children wanting to spend more time on devices is to interrupt the dopamine loop soon and often. In other words, we want to avoid the slot-machine effect of screentime.

Technology's persuasive design, not unlike the addictive chemicals found in food or drugs, is built to keep us using longer. But not all technology is built the same; there are sometimes better choices within our device or platform options and within the ways we engage with media. When you want to be intentional about how you or your children use screens, assess the available options as *best, okay,* and *worst.* Here are some examples:

> Best: Avoiding YouTube and YouTube Kids
> Okay: Watching YouTube or YouTube Kids in a common area
> Worst: Watching YouTube and YouTube Kids alone

> Best: Watching shows on a big TV in a common area
> Okay: Watching shows on a tablet in a common area
> Worst: Watching shows alone or with headphones

> Best: Avoiding apps that collect data about children
> Okay: Using paid versions of apps, which might still have persuasive design or gamification elements but will limit pop-up ads targeted at children or other annoying or addictive design features
> Worst: Using free versions of apps, which are usually lower quality and full of ads targeted at children

Once you've identified and ranked your tech choices on this three-point scale, lean toward selecting the best options as often as possible. This can help combat the impacts of persuasive design while interrupting the dopamine loop.

**For littles, this might look like the following:**

- Using the paid version of an app rather than the free version

- Testing apps or games out first and choosing those that do not use persuasive technology at all

- Whenever possible, choosing audio, a safer form of digital for kids because it doesn't manipulate attention in the same way as visual forms of technology and can be listened to while engaging in other forms of play (e.g., drawing or building with LEGO bricks)

**For middles, this might look like the following:**

- Educating them about the information apps collect and helping them see why this might be problematic later

- Helping them make choices within choices: If they want social media accounts, which ones are less problematic? If they want to watch YouTube, can they watch it in a common area? If they're using a personal device, does it stay out of their bedroom at night?

- Introducing them to other young activists who want to push back on Big Tech and showing them that they are not alone and there are ongoing efforts to change things

Taking our children to Las Vegas isn't in and of itself a bad idea; there are lots of great shows to see, fabulous lights and architecture, and fancy hotels. But if we take our children to Vegas, we're not going to drop them off in the casinos to wander on their own because the slot machines weren't built for kids. Similarly, screentime has its own entertainment value. But to keep our children safe, we must accompany and guide them as they navigate the internet and social media, limit them to the tech activities that actually align with our family values, model tech-intentional behavior, and set clear expectations and limits. And when they inevitably make mistakes or run into problematic content, we must be available to support, mentor, and problem-solve without judgment.

## Warning Sign #8: Deception

**Tech-intentional strategy: Own your mistakes.**
**Action: Use the power of repair.**

When we catch our children using the iPad without permission, they tend to come up with all kinds of excuses; my favorite is "I was picking lint off my sock. That's why it took me so long to come upstairs." It is developmentally normal for children to lie or act deceptively. But when it comes to problematic screen use, sneaking in screentime comes with a new set of risks and can lead to other stealthy behaviors online, which can have more serious consequences. So when we catch our kids being shifty, we don't want to come down hard on them or punish them. It won't change the sneaking; instead, it will drive it further underground.

Preempting our children's deceptive behaviors regarding tech use comes back to parental modeling and a concept called repair. This refers to owning our mistakes as adults and modeling honest behavior, which shows our children that we're not perfect and we have a responsibility to set things right again. When it comes to taking missteps when trying to manage screentime limits, we can go back and admit, "Oops. I messed up." We can also model apologizing—and, to be clear, saying, "I'm sorry you're so sensitive" is *not* an apology. Instead, saying, "Even adults mess up too, and I'm trying to do better. I am sorry I yelled at you" is clear and kind and shows that part of apologizing is taking responsibility for the hurt we may have caused, whether inadvertently or not.

Unfortunately, many of the ways in which we use screens can encourage sneaky behavior. For adults, this might look like using a filter on an Instagram picture to enhance our image or accepting the terms and conditions on a new app without reading them. When it comes to our children's use of screens, sometimes we lie on their behalf. For example, even though the federal Children's Online Privacy Protection Act states that kids have to be 13 or older to use the most popular platforms (e.g., YouTube, Instagram, and TikTok), many, many children under 13 are regular users. Either they were dishonest about their age when they signed up for it, or their parents signed up for them and lied about their age. And protecting our children from unsafe content online gets especially sticky when schools require preteens to use platforms like YouTube for homework or lessons—YouTube is restricted to ages 13 and older, and it's all too easy for younger children to end up in the wrong place if we're not paying attention to their screentime.

Our children will learn about honesty and online behaviors from watching how we interact with technology. Testing limits is normal. But when sneaky behavior is connected to screen and internet use, we need to be attentive. To help reduce our kids' temptation to be sneaky, we have to be adults who do not yell, punish, or shame them for the sneaky behavior in the first place.

**For littles, this might sound like the following:**

- "I know you want to use YouTube, but the law says kids have to be 13 or older to use it."

- "Oops, I made a mistake and let you play a game that wasn't for little kids. Let's find a game that is just right for your age."

- "I'm sorry that I yelled at you for sneaking the iPad. I want to talk about why we need you to ask permission to use it. It's about keeping you safe. That's part of my job as your parent."

**For middles, this might sound like the following:**

- "You are right that I spend a lot of time looking at my phone too. I hear you when you say that feels hypocritical. I'm going to try to be more aware of that. Thank you for letting me know how it makes you feel."

- "Part of my job as a parent is to keep you safe when you're online. Not everyone on the internet is trustworthy. That's why I ask you a lot of questions about what you're doing online. I always appreciate it when you share your experiences with me."

- "Why do you think it's important to represent ourselves honestly online? What do you notice when other people use filters in their posts? How does that make you feel?"

## Warning Sign #9: Using Screens to Escape or Relieve Mood

**Tech-intentional strategy: Don't use screens to punish or reward. Action: Find nondigital ways to address negative emotions or behaviors.**

Sometimes, screentime seems like the only thing that will help a child feel better. Adults are guilty of this too.

It is a fine balance. Watching reruns of the *Great British Baking Show* is going to have a more calming impact on our psyche compared with scrolling through influencer accounts on Instagram. And engaging in other activities besides screentime, such as playing board games, playing an instrument, or writing a short story, will affect our moods differently as well. Both research and anecdote bear this out:

as author Johann Hari puts it in his book *Stolen Focus*, "I don't like how I feel about myself after I spend a lot of time on social media. I like how I feel about myself after I spend a lot of time reading a book."

Curling up with a favorite show can be a comfort. But we need alternatives to screen-based means of escaping our problems or making ourselves feel better. Technology can't always be our default. Adults as well as children need coping strategies for when things in life feel hard.

"The only way out is through," a wise person once told me. And that means feeling our feelings and working through the hard moments. Doing so builds our confidence so that when future problems come up, we are prepared to handle them.

So if we want to avoid having our children turn to technology to self-soothe or escape, we have to teach them how to reflect on their emotions and apply analog strategies for mood relief, and we cannot use screentime to reward or punish. At first, it may seem effective to say, "If you don't do *X*, then you lose screentime," or "I'll give you extra screentime if you do *Y*," because such threats and incentives solve the problem *at the moment* by getting our child to comply with our request. But in the longer term, this strategy actually backfires and makes parenting experiences much more difficult. By instead identifying and providing nonscreen activities that comfort, soothe, distract, or motivate our children, we are setting them up for an adolescence and adulthood in which they will turn first to healthier coping choices instead of a device that will likely only bring them down more.

**For littles, this might look like the following:**

- Help your child name their feelings and identify things that help them feel better. Is it a comfort toy? Reading a book? A hug?

- Find something other than screentime to incentivize or react to behavior. This takes power away from screentime.

- Allow your child to be angry and upset without trying to fix it, but offer to be there to help if and when they need it. Remind them, "I know you can do hard things."

## For middles, this might look like the following:

- Keep the conversational doors open. For older kids, car rides are an opportunity to talk, in part because you're not facing each other, so it's less intense. (This is another good reason to limit or ban individual screen use in the car.)

- Offer and model opportunities to destress, relax, and unwind that do not involve screens, such as music, books, or exercise.

- Do not try to solve your adolescent's problems without their permission. Ask, "How can I support you?" or "Would you like me to just listen, or do you want some suggestions?"

- Do not use screens to reward or punish. If there is a safety issue that requires you to remove a device from a child, make it about the safety of the child, not about punishing them.

No parent wants to get to the end of their child's teen years and say, "What went wrong?" When we know the potential pitfalls of excessive screen use, we can take the necessary preventative steps now. The previous strategies are all rooted in building connection with and role modeling healthy habits and behaviors for our children.

Yes, this is a lot of work. Yes, it's mostly on us. And yes, we can do it.

There is one final strategy that I like to share that applies to any parenting challenge regarding screentime. We know that owning our mistakes is one important tech-intentional strategy. Similarly, a wise parent educator once taught me that it's not bad to admit we don't know everything. It's okay to tell our children, "I forgot to teach you that!" For example, when a child reacts in anger to something, we can say, "I forgot to teach you that we don't yell to get what we want." By owning our role as a parent to teach them what they need to know, the burden of responsibility shifts to the adult, who can use their more mature coping skills to handle it.

When it comes to screentime conflicts, the phrase "I forgot to teach you that" can be a powerful tool to turn down the heat. It gives us the opportunity to offer the gift of admitting we made a mistake, freeing up our children to possibly own their own—or at least appreciate that we prevented this conflict from going any further.

For tweens and teens especially, raging hormones make fights much more intense and emotional. That is developmentally normal. The biggest challenge for us as parents is not to take the bait, to keep our own emotions in check, and to remember that while our tweens and teens seem to hate us, they also still need us.

**For littles, "I forgot to teach you that" might look like this:**

- "I forgot to teach you that your brain really likes it when you play that game on the iPad. That's one reason it's so hard when it is time to turn it off!"

- "I forgot to teach you that it's not safe to chat with strangers on the internet. If someone you don't know sends you a message, it's really important you tell me about it so I can help!"

- "I forgot to teach you that social media is really for grown-ups, not kids. That's why we don't let you have your own account."

**For middles, "I forgot to teach you that" might look like this:**

- "I forgot to teach you that people think you're ignoring them when you look at your phone while someone is talking to you. It doesn't feel good to the other person."

- "I forgot to teach you that when you try to do homework while chatting online, you're dividing your attention, so it will take you way longer to get your work done."

- "I forgot to teach you that it's important to ask someone's permission before you take their picture. That's true for us as your parents too, so thanks for reminding us if we forget."

Working backward to go forward—that is, ensuring that our young children have analog alternatives to screens for learning, entertainment, and relief long before screentime issues become more problematic in their tweens and teens—means replacing judgment with curiosity and focusing on building, or rebuilding, the connection we have with our children. The solution to screentime addiction begins in the work we start today.

## TL;DR

- Children, especially teens, need autonomy, independence, and connection to thrive.

- Problematic screen use has many warning signs, and we should be on the lookout for them.

- There are many tech-intentional strategies and actions we can take to prevent screen use from becoming problematic.

- When it comes to screentime, human connection is the antidote to addiction.

# CHAPTER 8

# HOW TO BECOME TECH-INTENTIONAL

> There is no way to be a perfect parent—and a
> million ways to be a good one.
>
> —JILL CHURCHILL

**PARENTING ISN'T A LINEAR PROCESS.** Some choices we make are better than others. Even when focusing our efforts on becoming a firm and kind parent, we might veer too far toward permissive or authoritarian parenting on occasion.

It's okay. Successful parenting is about being comfortable with the uncertainty, the messiness, and the imperfections. It's about finding what works for our unique family, not what helped our sister's family or our neighbor's family. One-size-fits-all approaches to screentime don't work. We have to identify the changes that are realistic in light of *our* family's values and goals and concentrate on those. We must be okay with abandoning a strategy that doesn't work to see whether another one will. It means we don't compare our actions with what others are doing and remain focused on what works best for our children and our family. If we keep in mind that this is about progress, not perfection, we leave room for growth. We model for our children that parenthood is sometimes hard and that doing hard things is important.

Parenting in the digital age is about being a good-enough parent, not a perfect one. We cannot be great parents 100% of the time. I tell parents we are aiming for 80/20: 80% of the time, we're parenting within our values, prioritizing connection, and balancing our screen use. But 20% of the time, we're going to fall short. And that's okay because it's powerful for our children to see us work to strike a balance. As tech-intentional parents, we still argue with our child about screentime, but we also remember to repair—to explicitly own our mistakes—afterward. We make space for some screentime, but we ensure it is in sync with our child's development and our family's values. Recall that the definition of tech-intentional includes "using screen-based technologies that enhance, nurture, and support ourselves, our children, and our family in ways that align with our values and resisting, delaying, or limiting any type of screen use that interferes with our healthy mental, physical, cognitive, and emotional development." The application of this definition will vary from family to family, and conflicts will inevitably still arise, but it's how we cope with them that matters. We could also add to our definition, "As tech-intentional parents, we give ourselves room to try, fail, repair, and try again because it is in the mistake-making where we learn and grow."

Being tech-intentional is about so much more than implementing general rules about screentime. It's helpful to have a sense of which strategies work and don't, but setting specific limits must come *after* the work of becoming tech-intentional. Only after we are tech-intentional will those rules even stick or endure. So how do we become truly tech-intentional?

# THE SEVEN HABITS OF THE TECH-INTENTIONAL FAMILY

Not every family is the same. But the families who find balance with screen use often have several characteristics in common. What follows is a list of seven habits that tech-intentional families focus on.

## Habit #1: Trust the Concept of Good Enough

Much of our parenting journey is wondering if we are doing things right. We second-guess ourselves or compare our choices with those of other parents who seem to have it all together without really understanding that *all* parents experience uncertainty and that every child presents different challenges.

When we focus too much on being right, we lose sight of the value of being good enough. If we are overachievers or perfectionists, what we miss in trying to always achieve perfection is the value of the *process.* For example, we didn't learn to ride a bike on the first try. We had to fall, get up, and try again. As new parents, we often floundered in those first months or even years after bringing our babies home; we had to learn how to diaper, feed, sleep-train, and potty-train our infants and toddlers, and we didn't do it right every time. Similarly, as parents of older kids, we now must learn to navigate a world saturated in screentime, and being good enough means making mistakes in front of our children and showing them how we walk through fixing them. Normalize missteps; they are teachable moments. When we live our lives out loud, we're already doing this.

We are definitely not going to get it right each time. It's challenging, but we need to keep trying. Families who find success managing screentime in their household understand and live the adage that "perfect is the enemy of good"—meaning that pursuing the ideal has diminishing returns, gets in the way of doing good work, and does not achieve harmony. These families know that things will never be perfect, and they are okay with accepting that good enough is still good.

## Habit #2: Take Baby Steps

After a stressful argument or teen tantrum, parents rush to write a screentime contract, define device rules, and limit tech use—only to find that after three days of earnest effort, it all falls apart. If this sounds like you, you are not alone.

If you've tried this approach, it probably didn't work because when we try to define all the rules right out of the gate, we end up with a 20-page document that is impossible to maintain. Think about it: How often do you read the terms and conditions pages when you download a new app? Exactly: nobody does (though we probably should). Well-intentioned family screentime contracts are long, complicated, and hard to remember. They're not developmentally appropriate either; without reminders, lots of children forget to put their lunches in their backpacks or grab their soccer uniforms on their way out the door. A long list of screentime rules isn't going to stick either, especially if the children weren't a part of creating it.

To find success with limiting screentime in our households, we have to start small. When we try to change everything all at once, it doesn't work. But when we pick one small thing to change first, we are much more likely to have success. For our screen use, this might look like turning off the notifications on our own devices, charging our phones at night in a room other than the bedroom, or committing to a device-free meal once a week. With both screentime itself *and* trying to manage screentime, less is more, and change happens in small, incremental steps, not massive overhauls—in other words, baby steps.

## Habit #3: Uphold Your Family Values

Children rebel against rules because they don't understand them. This is logical: when something makes sense, it's easier to go along with. When it's confusing or complicated, we're more hesitant or resistant. So when we ground our parenting in the values we hold, our rules about media use are much more easily identified and enforced because they make sense.

When it comes to screentime, identifying the values we have as a family can help us define rules about device use that will be easy to understand and therefore easy to enforce. If you're still unsure of what your family's values are, then start with your nonnegotiables—the customs or routines your family already has—and work backward. For example, do you take your shoes off when you come into your house? Why? If it's because you don't want dirty shoes on the carpet, then you value taking care of your home. If you don't allow phones at the dinner table, then you value family conversation. Asking your kids, "What do you think is important to us in *our* family?" is another great way to identify your family's values.

Write down your top values, and post them visibly around the house. They can serve as conversation starting points and be referred to when talking about screen use. Use your values as a guide to teach about being tech-intentional.

## Habit #4: Avoid Comparing Yourself with Others

Social media increases our fear of missing out, or FOMO. But it also increases our concern that other families might be doing things better than we are. And keeping up with the one Jones family next door is hard enough; keeping up with all the Joneses on Instagram is impossible. Worrying about what other parents and families are doing increases our anxiety. I often say, "Twitter before bed messes with your head," meaning that doomscrolling through social media before bed never helps anyone sleep better. As the saying goes, "Don't let comparison be the thief of joy." Modified to reflect our increasingly digital lives, we might now say, "Don't let that one parent on Instagram make you feel bad about your kid's nonmonochromatic birthday party."

In other words, you need to do you. Don't waste time on comparison. We don't want our kids to think that other people's opinions influence us that significantly. We want to show our kids that being unique is a good thing. We want to build their confidence by encouraging them to do what feels right to them, not to act based on what others want, think, or say, especially online. As fellow tech-use expert Devorah Heitner says, we need to be their mentors, not just their monitors.

Ideally, this means we limit exposure to social media—for both kids and parents. There is plenty of research out there that too much time on social media isn't good for our mental health or social skills. We want to guide our kids in choosing healthy ways to express themselves confidently first rather than using social media to build—or (more likely) tear down—their confidence. And we can talk to them in neutral tones about this, using phrases like "I notice" and "I wonder" instead of criticizing their fascination with TikTok or Instagram. When it comes to limiting access to social media, remember that curiosity is disarming; judgment is not.

We aren't going to do the same thing as other families. That's okay. Celebrate the differences, and reinforce why your family does things the way you do.

## Habit #5: Take It Slow and Steady

In our fast-paced, instantly gratified world, we expect immediate change. We can check the news from all corners of the world at any hour of the day. We can download a movie to watch within seconds of picking it. We can message hundreds of friends with the tap of a screen.

But life doesn't move at the pace of technology; real life moves much, much slower, and the little moments matter. So when we want to make changes to family screentime, we must recognize and allow that it will take time. Screentime balance is not something we can order on Amazon Prime and get two hours later.

In a TEDx Talk titled "Children and Media," screentime expert and pediatrician Dr. Dimitri Christakis discusses how the pacing of children's shows has changed significantly during the past few decades. Many parents of my generation grew up with *Sesame Street* and *Mister Rogers' Neighborhood*; you can still watch reruns of these classic children's shows on YouTube. As Christakis points out, the pace of an old *Mister Rogers'* episode feels painfully slow today, but it is *developmentally* the pacing a young child needs. Current children's shows, by contrast, move at a much quicker pace, jumping between scenes and characters with rapid-fire dialogue and flashing images and colors. Christakis points out that when children engage with this faster-paced media for long enough, they start to expect that the real world should move at that pace too. And when it doesn't, they are bored.

As we know, boredom is an opportunity. But, as Kim John Payne, author of *Simplicity Parenting* and a former professor of mine from grad school, has noted, in our tech-saturated world, we start to shift the environment to fit our children's need for speed rather than slowing the environment down so that they can take the time they need to take in and process information in a way that matches their development.[32] This makes managing screentime even more difficult. So instead of allowing ever-faster media to shape our children's and our own realities, we may have to make different choices about how we

---

32   Kim John Payne, MEd, *Simplicity Parenting* (New York, NY: Ballantine, August 2010).

fill afternoons and weekends, say no more than we say yes, and build tech-free downtime into our schedules. This will allow us to adapt to our children's changing needs as they develop. I know it can feel like just as we master one developmental phase, we enter another, wholly unsure again. But we can include our children in this process of evolving. We can be ready to pivot and adapt.

Slowing down is not only okay; it's crucial.

## Habit #6: Delay, Delay, Delay

If you are still in the early stages of parenting or if you are wondering what the next steps are in getting children smart devices, let me share one comment that parents who've crossed that threshold *never* tell me: "I wish I had given my child a smartphone or social media sooner." Not a single parent has told me this. It is *always* the opposite: "I wish I had waited. I wish I had known then what I know now." If you're the parent of older children, you can share this message with those who have yet to hand over those devices or make the social media leap. And if you're the parent of younger children, ask those who've gone before you: "What do you wish you had known when you were in my position?"

One time, I was addressing a group of new parents and their infants. I spoke to the group for about 45 minutes, highlighting the importance of parent–child communication and relationships, how to be intentional about their own screen use, what to think about when taking and posting photos of children, communicating with relatives who lived far away, and so on. At the end, I asked if there were any questions. One mom raised her hand and said, "I have a comment. I thought today's discussion would be learning about when to introduce screens to our children. It never occurred to me to pay attention to how my husband and I use screens around our baby."

She was pointing out an important aspect of being tech-intentional: modeling healthy screentime behaviors has to start very early on in a child's life, and delaying or limiting access to screen-based media starts with assessing our own use of it.

Becoming tech-intentional is child specific and development dependent. What works for one family will not necessarily work for other families. But we all want to see our children grow, mature, and develop skills that will help them manage the inevitable stress that comes with having unlimited access to the internet and social media. And setting them up for that maturing and skill building means that we must start when our kids are young. That's because, from a big-picture perspective, childhood is brief—as the mother of a high schooler, I can certainly attest to the adage "The days are long, but the years are short." And what children need most are loving relationships with adults they trust, safe places to play outdoors, and opportunities to engage in creative play with other children—at all ages. It is through these experiences that they will build skills and resilience to better prepare for a future with digital devices—not through early access to or use of technology.

So remember to delay, delay, delay: delay early screentime access, delay the smartphone or smartwatch, and delay social media—for as long as possible.

## Habit #7: Worry About the Right Things

There are so many things that parents can worry about these days, and our constantly pinging news notifications provide real-time updates and more fodder for worry. It can be exhausting and overwhelming.

Too often, however, we worry about the wrong things. We get anxious about the mature vocabulary in song lyrics but ignore the message behind the words. We fret about our child seeing inappropriate content and delay smartphone access only to discover all their friends have phones and use them on the bus. We worry that our tween won't have friends or feel well liked, so we give in and allow them to create a social media account without equipping them with the tools or skills to use it in a healthy way, within the parameters of what is developmentally normal.

By contrast, parents who find success in navigating family screentime know to worry about the *right* things. They are guided by research-informed studies, not fear-based anxieties. They know to ask, "Tell me how this song makes you feel. Let's talk about it." When their children watch videos on their friends' phones, they have a conversation about what happens when their kids see something that makes them uncomfortable. And when their child wants to have a Snapchat account because they think they're the only one without it, these tech-intentional parents respond, "Let's explore what Snapchat's privacy policy states and see if it lines up with our family's values."

There are a lot of ways to have these conversations. The important thing is that we have them. Evaluating types of screentime is important too because it's not all the same: posting on social media, FaceTiming, gaming, and word processing are very distinct ways to spend time on a device. And a little bit of screentime is okay. For our children growing up in a highly digitized world, our worry should be focused on *excessive* screentime and waiting until our children are developmentally ready to have increased access. Parents must decide what we mean when we say, "It's too much."

## THE VALUES, RESPONSIBILITIES, AND PRIVILEGES OF BEING TECH-INTENTIONAL

Becoming a tech-intentional parent means working with your family to determine the values, responsibilities, and privileges that come with being a member of your household. This will look different for every family, but there are some common themes to keep in mind:

- All tech-intentional parenting strategies are rooted in family values.

- All members of a tech-intentional family are part of the process in deciding, establishing, enforcing, and modeling the limits or rules.

- All tech-intentional families leave room for making mistakes and growth.

- All tech-intentional parents know that they are the leaders of the family, not only in decision-making but also in modeling how screen-based technology is used.

Using the work you've done in previous chapters, it's now time to synthesize. With your family members, define the following:

1. What are the **values** that your family has identified as the most important? Aim for a low number (no more than four to five). Write these down as words, phrases, or statements.

   *Value Word Example:* Knowledge

   *Value Phrases Example:* Learning, togetherness, and fun

   *Values Statements Example:* We value learning. We love being together. We don't take things too seriously.

2. What are the **responsibilities** of each family member? Break these down into daily and weekly responsibilities per person. These will need to be appropriate for each stage of development, but even very young children can help put laundry away or pick up toys. Although you don't want to connect

doing chores to earning screentime, this list is simply what comes with the territory of living in your household. You do these things to take care of yourselves, your home, and one another. Parents can include themselves in this as well. Write these down.

*Example:* Daily chores for Child A: Put your backpack away, make your bed, and unload the dishwasher.

*Example:* Weekly chores for Child A: Vacuum upstairs, clean the bathroom, and do the laundry.

*Example:* Daily responsibilities for Parent A: Grocery shopping, cooking dinner, and managing schedules.

3. What are the **privileges** that come with being a member of your family? Some families might want to define weekend screentime versus weekday screentime. However you define it, be clear about what screentime refers to and how it fits into the privileges list. Additionally, use screentime as only *one* privilege among others that come with being a member of your family.

   *Example:* Children can have one hour of downtime watching their favorite show after school.

   *Example:* Children can alternate picking a game for family game night on Sunday evening.

   *Example:* On weekdays, children can have two hours of video game time.

   *Example:* Children get to spend one-on-one time with a parent in a shared nonscreen activity on Saturday afternoons.

For each family, the rules of screentime will look different, and that is okay.

Similarly, like technology, children grow and change, so you will have to revisit these lists periodically to touch base: How are things going? What's working? What isn't? What do you wish was different? How are you doing at holding up your end of your family's list of responsibilities? How are you feeling about the time you spend on screens?

## THE BENEFITS OF BECOMING A TECH-INTENTIONAL FAMILY

The first benefit of becoming a tech-intentional family is that we move away from being tech overwhelmed. It becomes possible to experience less conflict about screentime, decrease our stress levels, and watch our relationships blossom.

Second, being tech-intentional makes it possible to strike a balance with screentime. As our children grow up, we continue to adjust our limits and rules, but we always ground them within the values we have worked to establish. And this flexibility with clarity benefits us as well: tech-use balance is possible for us as adults too, whether that's setting a time of day to stop responding to work emails or taking our social media apps off our phone, and that can only improve our mental and emotional well-being.

Third, armed with information and knowledge about how excessive screentime impacts our children's development, we will make more confident choices about the limits we set. Rather than worrying or overreacting, as tech-intentional parents, we will see each new change in our child's development as another opportunity to revisit screentime limits and rules, and we will be able to adapt accordingly in a way that effectively safeguards our children.

Finally, as role models for healthy screen use, our choices, words, and actions show our children what kind of an adult we want them to grow up to be. By being tech-intentional, we will demonstrate to them the value of owning their mistakes, problem-solving, and staying true to their values—all important skills that will serve them, both online and off.[33]

## TL;DR

- Our children don't need perfect parents; they need good-enough parents.

- Tech-intentional families have seven habits in common:

  1. Trust the concept of good enough.
  2. Take baby steps.
  3. Uphold your family values.
  4. Avoid comparing yourself with others.
  5. Take it slow and steady.
  6. Delay, delay, delay.
  7. Worry about the right things.

- Tech-intentional families have clearly defined values, responsibilities, and privileges.

---

33    See Appendix C for the "Tech-Intentional Parenting Manifesto."

# EPILOGUE

# BE THE FIRST FISH

The only kinds of fights worth fighting are those
you're going to lose, because somebody has to fight
them and lose and lose and lose until someday,
somebody who believes as you do wins.

**—I. F. STONE**

**THIS BOOK OPENED WITH** the story of my former client, Carly, who was given an iPad as part of her school's one-to-one program. Through my conversations with Carly, I became acutely aware of the cart-before-the-horse problem we—and the education technology industry—were thrusting onto children in the name of 21st-century skills, innovation, or differentiation.

While most of these pages have focused on tech-intentional parenting, the elephant in the room is that screens for school have made the parenting side of this challenge much more difficult. A family with clear no-screens-before-bed rules is presented with a challenge when a child must upload a finished assignment to a learning management system. A teen who is not required to use a paper planner relies on their classroom webpage to look up homework. A teacher assigns a video to illustrate a concept for students to preview before class the next morning, requiring access to YouTube at home.

In a very short time and accelerated by remote learning during the pandemic, technology has seeped into education far more quickly than the legislation protecting children and their privacy has been able to keep up. My activism focuses on changing the law, pushing back on Big Tech in schools, and protecting children's data from the EdTech companies that profit from it. Schools and Big Tech are happy to push the burden of managing screentime onto parents (I often say that "EdTech is just Big Tech in a sweater vest"). To effect broader change, then, we will need to turn our attention to advocacy outside our homes too. That's because we can't wait for the laws to change. Our children will be grown and flown from the nest before legislation catches up or Big Tech decides to alter their business model in an impactful way.

Change starts at home, within our families, by becoming tech-intentional. Then, we must take what we've learned and bring it to the teachers, classrooms, and school boards and say, "Wait. Stop. This isn't right. It's not what's best for kids. Can we please talk about this?" Then, we can take the fight to our town and city governments, our state legislatures, and ultimately to the federal level.

Fighting for positive change when it comes to our children and technology can feel like playing digital Whac-a-Mole. Getting one technology company to improve parental controls is insignificant when others do not. Pulling one EdTech platform from a classroom while still relying on digital learning management systems makes our efforts seem futile. Convincing one parent to delay social media access when so many others give it readily makes it that much harder to stick to our choices. Nevertheless, we must keep pushing back, speaking up, and teaching others until the balance shifts. Our efforts, small but mighty, are planting the seeds now in hopes that later, enough people will see, understand, and help fight for change.

I spoke recently with Dr. Jared Cooney Horvath, an educational neuroscientist, who used a brilliant example to help us see why the power of a few can eventually tip the scales. "Take a school of fish," he explained. "When one fish swims away from the school, no other fish will follow. When two fish swim away, the school still won't follow. But after three or four fish, the school will shift direction." This fish story reminded me of my students. As a teacher, I watched my seventh graders go through all the typical growing pains of adolescent development: losing friends and making new ones; crushes and heartbreak; maturity and loss of childhood innocence. While I tried to make the curriculum as engaging and interesting as possible, what resonated with my students was talking about *them* and why the characters or stories we read were relevant to *their* lives.

In one lesson I taught regularly, I wanted to help my students understand the power of the bystander. When we talked about bullying, the focus was often on two people or parties: those doing the bullying and the target(s). As both an educator and now as a parent, I'd define bullying using the acronym *RIP*: bullying behaviors are *r*epeated, *i*ntentional, and involve a *p*ower imbalance. All three characteristics must be present to be considered bullying. It was abundantly clear to my students who had the social power in their grade. Usually a few socially powerful students wielded a lot of emotional control over the rest of the grade, and a few students were frequent targets.

As an exercise, on the whiteboard, I would draw two stick figures: one representing the bully, the other representing the target. Then, I'd ask my students, "How many stick figures do you see?" They'd answer correctly, "Two." Next, I'd ask, "How many students are in this classroom?" At the time, it was about 20; they'd answer correctly again. I'd then draw 18 more stick figures on the board. "Now," I'd ask, "which number is bigger: 18 or two?" My students would answer correctly, "18, of course."

Understanding would dawn on them as they looked at the size of the three groups of stick figures: one bully, one target, and 18 others standing by, watching. Granted, this was indeed a simplification: often, there are multiple kids with social powers who defer to a leader and more than one student who is a target; social dynamics are, after all, complex hierarchies. But I used this simplified illustration to clarify my point that while those who bully wield power, there is also power in numbers. When there are 16, 17, or 18 others watching another student exclude or humiliate another classmate, collectively, there can be power to stop that harmful behavior. The hard part, of course, is being that first fish to swim away from the group or that first bystander who can say, "Hey, wait a minute. That's not okay. Stop." That first fish or student can then draw the second, the third, and ultimately the rest of the group toward another path.

Horvath called this a threshold: a point at which there are enough people doing something to change direction, such as swimming toward a new destination, speaking up against bullying behaviors, pushing back on Big Tech, or resisting EdTech in the classroom. Until that threshold, most people don't feel safe; therefore, nothing will change. "We can't convince people solely with data," he said. "We can't do this alone."

Being the first fish feels vulnerable, which is why many people so often do nothing. With social media and 24/7 news, we see, hear, and read about all the bad things that happen to people who dare to speak up or push back. We can read the hate-filled messages online trolls post in comment threads. But remember that scary is not the same thing as dangerous. It is scary to stand up to a person with more social power than we have; it is dangerous to watch them perpetuate

harm on others. It is scary to push back on Big Tech; it is dangerous to let them profit off our children. It is scary to ask our child's
school to offer a nonscreen alternative; it is dangerous to expect our
children to learn as well on computers or tablets. It is scary to delay
social media access and have our teen think we're the worst parent
in the world; it is dangerous to give our children unlimited access to
platforms that weren't designed for them.

Doing hard things is scary. If we want to learn a new skill, we can't
just practice the skills we already know because we won't improve.
If we want to become a better athlete, we can't do the same exercise
routine and expect change. If we choose to stay quiet or wait for others to speak up, the status quo remains.

Michelle Obama once said on an episode of *The Late Show with
Stephen Colbert* that the moment in her life when she felt most
afraid was when Barack told her he wanted to run for president.
She knew that everything about their life would change. It would
mean leaving their hometown, their house, their friends, and putting their family on a very public stage. It felt scary to think about
doing this, and she knew that if she said she didn't want him to run,
he wouldn't. But she also knew that if she made that call from a
place of fear, they couldn't be a voice for change. They couldn't fight
for the causes they cared about. They couldn't advocate for those
who had previously been denied a voice.

As the former first lady pointed out, she could have said no and
made that huge decision rooted in her fear. If she had, American his-
tory would be very, very different today. Groups whose voices needed
to be heard might not have been given an opportunity to speak.
People whose power seemed infinite might have gone unchallenged.
It is scary to do hard things. But doing nothing is dangerous.

We may not be Michelle Obama, but we all make hard decisions. When our decisions are rooted in fear and anxiety, we remain

stagnant. When our choices are based in research, values, and trust, we grow. This is especially true when it comes to raising our children and managing their screentime.

It will take courage to be the parent who says no to smartwatches, smartphones, and social media. It will take strong self-regulation to be yelled at by our children who want more gaming time. It will take confidence to say to our schools, "This isn't what is best for children." And even beyond facing our children's disappointment, frustration, or anger, we are up against enormous other pressures—not just from Big Tech but from other parents too. So many have fallen prey to the thinking that their children need tech to be successful or that their tween needs a smart device to have a social life.

But they're wrong. What we are already seeing and will continue to see is growing evidence that the harms of screen use, especially social media, outweigh its rare benefits. We have already seen the U.S. Surgeon General declare social media a "driver of the current youth mental health crisis."[34] We will witness more lawsuits against social media companies for preying on young children's vulnerabilities. We will watch as more hatred and misinformation spread through online channels. And we will see Congress—hopefully, eventually, finally—act. In the meantime, it is our battle to fight.

This is perhaps the most important thing we will do as parents today: ensure a technological future that will value and protect our children's emotional, mental, and cognitive health, prioritize people before profits, and place love before likes. This is our call to action: you are not alone. This is a fight worth having. Be the first fish.

We can do this.

---

34    U.S. Department of Health and Human Services, "Surgeon General Issues New Advisory About Effects Social Media Use Has on Youth Mental Health," May 23, 2023, https://www.hhs.gov/about/news/2023/05/23/surgeon-general-issues-new-advisory-about-effects-social-media-use-has-youth-mental-health.html.

# ACKNOWLEDGMENTS AND GRATITUDE

My business coaches, my writing coaches, my mindset coaches, my colleagues and allies, my clients, and my therapist—thank you.

My Screentime Consultant teammates—I couldn't have done this without your talent, skills, and kindness.

My activism buddies, who know the long fight is worth the effort.

My team at Greenleaf, who took this book from good to great.

My siblings, cousins, extended family, and family friend network; for the IRL connections that make life far more interesting.

My friends from far and wide, who still pick up the phone to call, who have cheered me on, who make me laugh.

My in-laws, for their continued love, support, and encouragement.

My parents, for giving me an 80s childhood full of messy play, trees, the occasional movie or TV show, and for always believing in me.

My teachers, who deeply impacted the trajectory of my life. I am here because of you.

All my former students, for being my best teachers.

And of course, Ben, Max, Sylvie, and Penny—my best sources of dopamine.

# APPENDIX A

**Technology Today Is Not Technology from Yesterday**

| Activity | Characteristics | Gen X (1980s childhood) | Gen Z (2010s childhood) | What we lost |
|---|---|---|---|---|
| WATCHING A TV SERIES | Variety of programming | Very limited programming | Numerous options per streaming provider | A lack of options (we are overwhelmed by choices now) |
| | Number of devices | One television per household | One device per child | The skill of negotiating programming choices as a household |
| | Availability | Aired on one station at one day and time | On-demand streaming, 24/7 | Shared viewing experiences |
| | Schedule | Weekly episodes with off seasons that lacked new programming | As many episodes in one sitting as allowed; new content always available | The need to wait (the skill of delaying gratification) |
| | Content source | Content determined by focus groups | Suggested content (and ads!) determined by user history | Boredom (reruns or nothing to watch) and data privacy |
| | Method of watching | Viewing together as a family, in one room, with few distractions | Viewing individually, on separate devices or even in different rooms, with multiple distractions | Focused family time and shared experiences |

*continued*

| Activity | Characteristics | Gen X (1980s childhood) | Gen Z (2010s childhood) | What we lost |
|---|---|---|---|---|
| WATCHING A MOVIE | Number of devices | One television per household | One device per child | The skill of negotiating programming as a household |
| | Variety of choice | Viewing options limited to availability of movie rentals | Numerous options per streaming provider | The need to wait or limit consumption (the skill of delaying gratification) |
| | Amount of parental supervision | Content negotiated as a family and often limited by a parental figure | Parental controls that children work around | The knowledge of what our kids are watching |
| | Method of watching | Viewing together as a family at the movie theater or in one room at home, with few distractions | Viewing individually, on separate devices or even in different rooms, with multiple distractions | Focused family time and shared experiences |

*continued*

| Activity | Characteristics | Gen X (1980s childhood) | Gen Z (2010s childhood) | What we lost |
|---|---|---|---|---|
| PLAYING VIDEO GAMES | Cost | One-time purchase | Endless opportunities for purchasing upgrades (e.g., maps, skins, weapons, and upgrades) | Control of our credit cards due to constant upselling |
| | Game play | Console based (local) | Online (decentralized) | Control of the content our children have access to |
| | Online social interaction | Cooperative interactions limited to controller and game options | Competitive interactions with players of all ages across the globe (a.k.a. total strangers) | Supervision of who our children are gaming with |
| | Complexity | Limited content storage and graphics ability | Open-world maps with endless quests | Limited game play |
| | Advertising | No ads | Pop-up or in-game ads for additional games or downloadable content | Limited access to new gaming options |
| | In-person socializing | Friends coming over to play in person | Playing alone, with friends in a different house, or with strangers | Authentic communication and relationships |

# APPENDIX B

**Ages and Stages of Development**

**THE FOLLOWING TABLE PRESENTS** Jean Piaget's stages of development and key developmental milestones, recommendations regarding media use by the World Health Organization (WHO)[35] and American Academy of Pediatrics (AAP),[36] tech-intentional tips we can use as parents regarding screentime, and questions we can ask to ensure that our child is developing optimally.

| Age or stage | Piaget's stage of development | WHO/AAP recommendations | Tech-intentional tips | Questions to ask |
|---|---|---|---|---|
| INFANTS AND TODDLERS (BIRTH–TWO YEARS OLD) | **Sensorimotor**<br><br>Learns about their world through movement and touch<br><br>Understands that they are a separate being from other people or objects<br><br>Recognizes that their actions can cause things to happen<br><br>Understands object permanence (i.e., things still exist even when they go away)<br><br>Develops early language skills through interactions with caregivers | **WHO:**<br>No exposure to screens<br><br>**AAP:**<br>Before 18 months, avoid media exposure, except video chatting. After age 18 months, high-quality programming co-viewed with parents | Prioritize face-to-face communication.<br><br>Minimize and delay screentime.<br><br>Allow FaceTime with relatives.<br><br>Encourage hands-on, tactical, 3D play.<br><br>Live life out loud (see chapter 4).<br><br>Connect whenever possible. | Is my child getting enough sleep?<br><br>Is my child moving around in a variety of ways throughout the day?<br><br>Is my child hitting developmental milestones?<br><br>Is my child communicating with me nonverbally?<br><br>Is my child connecting with caregivers? |

*continued*

35  World Health Organization (WHO), https://www.who.int/.

36  American Academy of Pediatrics (AAP), https://www.aap.org/.

| Age or stage | Piaget's stage of development | WHO/AAP recommendations | Tech-intentional tips | Questions to ask |
|---|---|---|---|---|
| **PRESCHOOL/ KINDER- GARTEN (TWO–SEVEN YEARS OLD)** | **Preoperational**<br><br>Understands that words and pictures represent objects (symbolic thinking)<br><br>Is egocentric and finds it hard to take the perspective of others<br><br>Thinks concretely<br><br>Struggles with logic and point of view<br><br>Develops language skills | **WHO:**<br>No more than one hour per day of sedentary screen use<br><br>**AAP:**<br>No more than one hour per day of high-quality programming co-viewed with adults | Encourage kids to read, read, read.<br><br>Talk about feelings and expressing them.<br><br>Establish family values (see chapter 2).<br><br>Introduce media literacy skills.<br><br>Do not use or allow digital devices at mealtime or bedtime.<br><br>Use clear, direct, and simple directions.<br><br>Notice, name, and appreciate (e.g., "When you do X, then you can have Y"). | Is my child getting enough sleep and exercise?<br><br>Is my child engaged in nonscreen-related activities?<br><br>Is my child read to daily?<br><br>What family values are most important to us, and how does technology fit in?<br><br>As parents, do we model healthy tech use? |
| **ELEMENTARY SCHOOL (SEVEN– ELEVEN YEARS OLD)** | **Concrete operational**<br><br>Thinks more logically and in a more organized way; continues to think very concretely<br><br>Starts to use reasoning (inductive logic)<br><br>Gets better at thinking about other points of view<br><br>Struggles with abstract and hypothetical concepts | **WHO:** N/A<br><br>**AAP:**<br>Limit time and type of media, and prioritize sleep and exercise.<br>*Note: No current recommendations on screens for school.* | Build executive function skills.<br><br>Take perspective.<br><br>Encourage kids to read, read, read.<br><br>Be savvy consumers.<br><br>Support screen-free activities.<br><br>Teach children about persuasive design.<br><br>Delay smartphones.<br><br>Set clear, consistent limits about screen use.<br><br>Make consequences time relevant and concrete. | Is my child getting enough sleep and exercise?<br><br>What nonscreen activities does my child participate in?<br><br>What screen-based requirements does my child's school require, and how can I push back?<br><br>What screentime limits are other families setting, and how can we support each other? |

*continued*

Appendix B

| Age or stage | Piaget's stage of development | WHO/AAP recommendations | Tech-intentional tips | Questions to ask |
|---|---|---|---|---|
| MIDDLE SCHOOL (ADOLESCENCE) | **Formal operational**<br><br>Develops abstract thinking<br><br>Reasons about hypotheticals<br><br>Understands moral and philosophical issues<br><br>Develops deductive logic<br><br>Sees multiple potential solutions<br><br>Is able to plan for the future | **WHO:** N/A<br><br>**AAP:**<br>Limit time and type of media, and prioritize sleep and exercise.<br>*Note: No current recommendations on screens for school.* | Mentor, don't just monitor.<br><br>Prioritize safety and privacy.<br><br>Consider a "dumb" phone.<br><br>Push back on screens for schools.<br><br>Put skills before screens.<br><br>Prioritize executive function skills.<br><br>Model the behavior you want to see.<br><br>Set and enforce limits.<br><br>Connect whenever possible. | Is my tween/teen getting enough daily sleep and exercise?<br><br>If screens are required for school, how do we push back, and how do we set limits?<br><br>Does my child know our phone numbers, address, how to get home from school, and what to do in an emergency—without the use of a smartphone? |
| HIGH SCHOOL AND BEYOND | N/A | **WHO:** N/A<br><br>**AAP:**<br>Limit time and type of media, and prioritize sleep and exercise.<br>*Note: No current recommendations on screens for school.* | Encourage mastering basic life skills.<br><br>Prioritize sleep and self-care. | Is my teen getting enough sleep?<br><br>Does my teen complete tasks without being asked?<br><br>Does my teen have family responsibilities?<br><br>Does my teen engage in nonscreen activities? |

205

# APPENDIX C

### Tech-Intentional Parenting Manifesto

*Adapted from Brené Brown's "Wholehearted Parenting Manifesto"*

Above all else, we want you to know that we love you no matter what.

Being a kid (and a parent) in the digital age is *hard*. It's hard for you as a kid, and it is hard for us as parents. Things change faster than we can keep up with. We want you to know that our efforts to set limits on screen use reflect our deep desire to both protect you and nurture you as you grow.

We want you to engage with the world—the *real* world. We want you to see the beauty and the mess, the chaos and the calm, and we want you to see yourself as an important part of that. We want you to observe us, your parents, valuing time spent in nature, in conversation with people, and in activities that do not require a screen. We want you to know that it is possible—and indeed wonderful—to find joy in these things.

As a family, we will build courage by doing hard things, like prioritizing relationships by delaying access to smartphones and social media, setting and modeling limits, and asking questions about screen use in school settings. We will approach these as your team-mates and allies, not your enemies or adversaries. We know that we're fighting to protect your future mental, emotional, and cogni-tive health. We will include you in that fight and help you understand why it is so important.

We will be parents who assess and reassess our *own* use of screen-based technology and hold ourselves to the same standards. We will look closely at our use of personal devices for work, socializing, enter-tainment, and household management. We will be humble when our own tech use interferes with our values or relationships. We will be willing and open to feedback and change.

We will trust you, but know that we do not trust all things online. We trust you to tell us when you see something that scares you or makes you uncomfortable, and you can trust that our reaction will not be to punish or shame. We appreciate honesty and will always offer our support in problem-solving.

We recognize that many young people find virtual communities of connection. We want you to find communities offline, but we also understand that eventually, some of those experiences may be online. When that happens, we hope that you will find ways to balance real life with digital life, real friendships with virtual ones.

We will not always find this a smooth path. There will be many zigs and zags, and we will make mistakes. So will you. Mistakes are a part of life. We want to help you see mistakes as opportunities for growth and change, not as failures or deficits. We hope that you see our mistakes as trial and error too, while we figure out how to parent in this unprecedented era.

In our family, being tech-intentional means using screen-based technologies that enhance, nurture, and support us. It means resist-ing, delaying, or limiting screen use that interferes with healthy mental, physical, cognitive, and emotional development. It means learning about resilience and strength by making choices in alignment with our values, not from our anxieties or fears.

We are tech-intentional because we love you and we want you to love the world you are an important part of.

# COMMON FAQS

**Q: I played video games and watched TV when I was a kid, and I'm fine. Why should I worry now?**

A: TV and video games looked very different when you and I were kids. We had to wait a week for the next episode, and our shows were only available at certain days and times, which made it easier to stop watching when shows were over. Video games were also much less sophisticated. Today, game designers use behavior-driving techniques to purposefully hook people and keep them playing. In other words, the deck is stacked against our kids much more than it was against us.

**Q: My kid says they are bored and the only thing that will make them happy is screentime. What should I do?**

A: Tell them, "I have a bathroom for you to clean," and they may find something to occupy their time. If that doesn't work, ask whether they would like some suggestions about what to play with or how to occupy their time. Kids often ask for screentime because they don't have to solve the problem of boredom. However, boredom is so important for their brain development and creativity. If they are stuck and not sure what to do next, give them a few choices, and ask them to try at least one for a few minutes. They may need to rebuild that creative muscle if they haven't used it in a while.

**Q: How much screentime is too much?**
A: My not-so-satisfying answer to this often-asked question is "A little is okay, and a lot is too much." We must remember that not all device use is created equal and that each child responds differently to different experiences. The concern is not a little bit of screen-time; it's *excessive* screentime. The American Academy of Pediatrics recommends that for infants (zero to 18 months), avoid all digital media except video chatting; for toddlers (18 to 24 months), co-view all screentime; and for ages two to five years, limit screen use to one co-viewed hour a day of high-quality programming. The organization says nothing about tech-use guidelines for children over age six; that's up to parents! For each family and each child, this will look different.

**Q: Which parental control apps do you recommend?**
A: None. I don't recommend parental control apps because kids are very good at figuring out ways around them.

**Q: My kid keeps telling me everyone else has a phone. What should I say?**
A: "No, they don't."

**Q: Phones keep my kids safe, and I use parental controls. Why should I worry?**
A: Phones do not make children safer. Indeed, they make them less safe. Parental controls are a Band-Aid, not a solution. If you have parental controls or filters that you like, then use them. But we need to mentor our kids, not just monitor them. Even with filters and

controls, kids find stuff. If you aren't comfortable with that, your children probably aren't yet ready to be unsupervised smartphone users.

**Q: What if my spouse, coparent, or other family members have different values?**
A: That's normal and completely okay. It's a great way to show your kids that two people who don't agree on everything can still be great parents and caregivers! The goal is to find common ground. Even if it's something really small, start there; then build.

**Q: My kid is obsessed with their phone, but they keep throwing my own phone use at me. I'm an adult. This is a kid problem, isn't it?**
A: Screen overuse isn't a kid problem; it's an adult problem. Kids model the behaviors they see in their parents, which means if we want to see them change their behavior, we need to take a really honest look at our own.

**Q: Okay, I get it: I need to look at my own screen use. Are there some quick tips for reducing my own screentime?**
A: Yes! Making the screen less attractive by using grayscale or turning off notifications will reduce your time on your phone. My YouTube channel features a series called *Tech-Intentional Tips*, which are short videos with more specific actions you can take to reduce your tech use.

**Q: My kids need technology to be prepared for the future, don't they?**
A: How many times have you thought to yourself in a meeting, "Wow, I'm so glad I learned that lesson on Oregon Trail"? Seriously, though, the technology we have today probably won't look like what our children use during their day jobs years from now. They also need several skills that can't be developed using a screen. The best preparation for

a career isn't time on tech; it is time spent building executive function skills, such as planning, prioritization, organization, emotion regulation, and cognitive flexibility.

**Q: My kid refuses to use a planner for school and says they can "just look it up online." How do I make them use one?**

A: First of all, we can't make our kids do anything. But we can invite them to experiment. Suggest to your child that they try to not rely on the school's learning management system to track homework for one week. Be curious; say, "I wonder whether this will make it easier or harder to track your assignments." Keep in mind also that kids have to find an organizational system that works for them, not for you. So take them to the office supply store and look at how different planners are set up. What format appeals to them? Modeling the behavior helps too: use a family whiteboard or shared paper calendar where you can see everyone's activities and schedules.

**Q: It seems like my child's friends only want to come over to play if they can use screen-based devices. What should I do?**

A: This is where our work as tech-intentional parents may differ from that of other families. That's okay. Using the values you've established around screen use, talk with your child about what nonscreen-based activities might be of interest if other children were to come over. If it aligns with your screentime values, select a part of the playdate to include shared gaming or screentime, but balance it with other activities. Strive to make your home a place other kids get to do fun things they miss out on by being on screens all the time. We can also show empathy to our child and acknowledge their feelings. It helps to find other parents who share your view and focus on building relationships between your families to reinforce and normalize your choices.

**Q: During the pandemic, all our screentime rules went out the window. How do I start to establish new limits now?**

A: By living your life out loud, meaning you express why you're using your device as you're using it and how you're feeling at the time. Yes, it can feel awkward and weird at first, but the more you practice it, the more comfortable it becomes. And you can do this even when your children are preverbal; in fact, that's the best time to start! You cannot change everything all at once and expect things to stick. Start with the low-hanging fruit: live your screentime life out loud.

**Q: I do a great job of managing my own screentime. It's my spouse who has the real issues and doesn't agree with me at all. What should I do?**

A: This is a challenge. When two parents don't agree on a topic, kids pick up on that tension. The goal here is to start with values (see chapter 3) and find common ground. It may mean focusing on something other than screentime, such as prioritizing a family activity. Tech use is a heated issue, and parents also feel judged. If we want to make meaningful changes that last, however, we do have to address our own use first. Refrain from judging one another, and find ways to ask for support. All this problem-solving is great modeling for your kids too. Disagreeing isn't necessarily bad; it's how you resolve your differences and find common ground that matters.

**Q: What should I do when my child calls me out for not living my life out loud?**

A: Celebrate! Say, "Thank you for noticing!" If your children are rolling your eyes at you every time you live your life out loud, you know it is impacting them—they are listening. And if they call you out on it, don't get defensive. Take a deep breath, and appreciate the feedback.

The more you do it, the more they will see and hear it, and hopefully, they will start to emulate your behavior. The best outcome is that our children start living their lives out loud too. But remember, it starts with us.

**Q: Why is it so hard for my kid to put down their screens?**
A: Because of persuasive design. These products influence our neural pathways, causing us to want more and more screentime to achieve the same level of pleasure. Persuasive design affects people of all ages, but children's brains are not adult brains; they are more susceptible to these design elements. Give yourself grace: it's not a fair fight, and it is not at all like when we were kids and watched a lot of TV.

**Q: Is there anything I can do to avoid the meltdown my kid has after I limit access to screens?**
A: Unfortunately, that meltdown is a chemical response triggered by our interrupting the different reward signals their brains get by interacting with a device. Kids haven't developed enough executive function skills yet to rationalize their way through the withdrawal. You can, however, plan for the tantrum by having alternative means of occupying their time ready to suggest and going in with a game plan.

**Q: My kid has great judgment. Do I need to worry about excessive screen use?**
A: Yes. Our brains aren't fully developed until well into our 20s. Kids need adults to help them set boundaries and model healthy behavior.

**Q: When should I get my kid a smartphone?**
A: When you are ready for them to see content that contains, for example, pornography, violence, cyberbullying, hate, and eating disorders. If you're not ready for them to see that, they're not ready for a personal

device (and remember: parental controls don't catch everything; see chapter 2). So here's a pro tip: test the waters yourself first by creating a fake account on whatever platform or app you're considering allowing your child to have. Try it for a week, and see whether it's something you'd feel comfortable letting your child have access to.

**Q: I don't feel connected to my kid at all. They never seem interested in doing anything with me. What should I do?**

A: This will take a lot of small efforts. Don't focus on big activities or events; instead, find the little things you can connect over. Additionally, if your child is feeling particularly defensive, it may be because you've previously given them the message that you don't approve of their choices. Try to soften your reactions. Replace judgment with curiosity: ask about what they're interested in, even if it is something on a screen. Find a starting point; then, build from there.

**Q: My child is definitely addicted to screens. What should I do?**

A: Unfortunately, there are some children (and adults) for whom screen addiction is a very real thing. It's really important to seek professional support, starting with your pediatrician. Don't rely on parental controls or apps to try to pull things back. The tools you need are beyond the purview of this book. For more information about screen addiction, search online for reSTART, which provides professional counseling and therapy for behavioral disorders related to problematic screen use.

**Q: Screentime is the only thing I can use to motivate my kids. What else can I do?**

A: This is a good indication that the balance has tipped too heavily toward screens as something that has a lot of power in your household. Start by slowly reintroducing other activities into the daily routine before you change your strategy of using screentime to motivate. This is an area where you may have to work backward to go forward by introducing analog activities as early in your child's life as possible.

**Q: How long should I delay access? What's best and what's realistic might be two different things.**

A: In an ideal world, no child should have a smartphone, smartwatch, or social media until late high school. That's based on what we know about child development, optimal learning, and mental health. However, it's true that this may not always be realistic. No parent has regretted waiting; many have regretted giving devices too soon. It is much, much harder to take away than it is to delay. Being clear is kind. If you want to delay, tell your kids, "We won't get phones until eighth grade or social media until age 16." It is always easier to lower that age limit than it is to raise it. Give yourself room.

**Q: This is all well and good, but screens for school have made our family life so much harder. How do we address that?**

A: I am with you on this. The reliance on EdTech really has complicated things. It's hugely problematic, it's rarely developmentally appropriate, and it's often disruptive to learning. Changes can come from the top down (but they will be slow, if they ever occur). But they can also come from the bottom up. This means parents speaking up and speaking out about screen use for school. For more information, use tools like EverySchool.org, Fairplay for Kids, and the Student Data Privacy Project.

# ABOUT THE AUTHOR

**EMILY CHERKIN, MEd,** The Screentime Consultant, is a nationally recognized consultant who takes a tech-intentional™ approach to addressing screentime challenges. A former middle school teacher, she has been featured for her work in the *New York Times* and the *Washington Post*, as well as on the *Today Show* (twice), *Good Morning America, Australia Weekend Today,* the BBC, NPR, Sirius XM Radio, and numerous parenting websites, blogs, and podcasts. Chuck Norris has quoted her. Emily teaches parenting courses, offers private parent consultations, facilitates professional development training, gives keynote speeches and corporate presentations, and provides personalized school presentations built on her tech-intentional approach. As a parent to a twelve- and fifteen-year-old, Emily understands deeply the real-life challenges of parenting in the digital age. Emily is also the cofounder of the Student Data Privacy Project, an advocacy group focused on protecting schoolchildren's data. More can be found at www.thescreentimeconsultant.com.